jessica**Care**moore

GOD
IS NOT AN
AMERICAN

poetry, **politics** & *love*

Publisher Contact: 313 974 5111
For bookings, sales.
mooreblackpressinfo@gmail.com

Cover Design: Michael Angelo Chester
michaelangelochester@gmail.com
Cover Photography of Author: Jerry Taliaferro
From Women of a New Tribe Exhibit
Back Cover Photo: Corey Reese
corey.reese@gmail.com

Edited by: **Moore Black Press Staff**
Editorial Assistance: Chantay Leonard and 1st Draft Edit, Raven Jones

Other Moore Black Press Books
by jessica Care moore:
The Words Don't Fit in My Mouth
The Alphabet Verses The Ghetto.

Copyright 2009 Moore Black Press
Detroit, Michigan 48208

Moore Black Press Inc.
Dedicated to legacy since 1971

Jessica Care Moore's poems—fearless, resilient words with such real muscle—have continually spoken to and helped define a generation of urbanistas and our brothers, lovers, daddies, cousins and homies. Once again she does not disappoint.

With **God is Not an American** *she pushes us, pulls us, coaxes and calls us along with her on the rides of our lives: the rough, smooth, sexy, ugly, beautiful, rich, impoverished, kind and mean rides. Here she reminds us of the absolute power of and need for authenticity in any creative process. And I, for one, am both ever grateful and more, renewed.*

—asha bandele
Author, *Something Like Beautiful* and *The Subtle Art of Breathing*

"I pray your voice is never bought, owned, silenced, censored, or dimmed"
—Ernie Paniccioli
Legendary Hip Hop Photographer

"The Beyonce of Poetry"

—Don Vest
Broadside Press

In Memory of

Yale Guy Miller (Njoma)

and always my daddy,

Thomas Davis Moore

the book, according to jessica

Thank you to the Moore Family, my extended family
(you know who you are), friends, fellow artists, all you beautiful
poets, activists, educators, and musicians across the world, single
mothers, survivors, and ancestors.

I am grateful for your presence in my life.

Thank you God
Allah
& the Sun, the Ocean, the Trees and the Wind
The Orishas.
& all Women Who Run With Wolves.

Thank you to my birth son

King Thomas James Moore Poole

You are all the poems I'll ever need.

A STORM IS COMING: AN INTRODUCTION

A positive aspect of poets is that they think too much. They attach themselves to ideas, moments and movements that unsettle the comfort zones of the rulership. In finding their voices, the best of them often steal the smiles of others while claiming the oneness of the human heart. Poets, more often than not, the world over are living poor, no check to no check, always broke, forever searching for rent, food and clothing money, looking for publishing opportunities, hunting for reading gigs, and yet, deep in the residue of their interiors their tears come like waterfalls. They, the poets, the best of them, love over much and collect the pain of those unaware souls rushing toward the gigantic hurt awaiting all of us.

Jessica Care Moore is a wanderer with a middle name that defines her spirit and that will forever light difficult paths for her. In her latest collection *God is Not an American: Poetry,* Politics & Love, she navigates new boundaries and territories that forever stretches her young and engaging mind. She walks among stones and storms, volcanoes, hurricanes and raindrops falling on her head and men, always men, telling her how pretty she is. I've heard this story before. Yellowblack women whose beauty could stop buses, trains and airplanes flown by blind pilots; yellowblack women distrusted by men who could never handle beauty or women smarter than they, because they had been seasoned from birth to hate themselves.

Yes, I know this urban tale, this all too common tragedy always searching for a happy ending. Yet, there is something different and magnificent here. In her house there is a king present, dropped from Ms. Moore's insides that saved and redirected her life. King, her son speaks a language only mothers can comprehend. King informed his mother that the color of love is complex, confirmed that living is also hard memory, is deep lines in the palm of her writing hand, is learning to box without hitting a speed bag, is absorbing concentrated attacks from strangers for no reason other than that you are different, talented, a misunderstood wordsmith with a functioning brain; a yellowblack woman who dares to speak volumes as a poet.

Remarkable magic is Jessica Care Moore, who has crafted a book not unlike the compositions of our best musicians. She sings in her own language, cadence and style dancing on the page, demanding that we consider a life, her life, which is attached to so many other lives. So much of this volume is autobiographical; this book is five years in the making, carrying us to Europe, South Africa and numerous cities in the United States, then ending from where she started in Detroit, Michigan.

The musical quality of her work is early Motown, however her lineage, her pedigree is actually poet and publisher of Broadside Press Dudley Randall, is poet and publisher of Lotus Press Naomi Long Madgett, is the insightful and brilliant eyes of playwright Ron Milner; the staying power and talent of the producer, director, and fiction writer Woodie King, Jr., the political accruement and dedication of Malcolm X, the range and craft of Aneb House; and the drive, commitment and seriousness of the young Don L. Lee. As the poet and publisher of Moore Press, she has maintained and is building on the grand tradition that Detroiters have placed at the doorstep of the world. She writes, "There has to be something other than ego in it, there has to be a gift to publishing."

However, everything starts with the word; her poetry is where we must begin. It is in the quality of her eye and the focus of her sharp imagination that separates her from the multitude of writers crowding Starbucks and MFA programs. She is a reader and happily stands on the shoulders of those masters who preceded her. It is they who she pays homage to that helps us to understand her, acknowledges the poet in her. In this powerful collection Lucille Clifton is here, Amiri and Amina Baraka teach her, Ossie Davis' voice is magnified, Kalamu ya Salaam is a safe place; there is a praise song for Sekou Sundiata; as well as a glimpse of Tupac's genius, Sonia Sanchez' survival strategies. Of Elaine Brown, Juanita Abernathy, Evelyn Lowery and Kathleen Cleaver, women of the Civil Rights Movement she writes:

you

represent

the project monifa

the double-dutch champion

hopscotch heroin

voodoo candy lady

tree-limbed traffic stopper

the bubble gum popper

the pigtailed astronomer

everybody's baby mama

the storm calmer

a father's daughter

the birth of blues

queen of queens

you.

goddess

you.

warrior.

i am certain

none of us

would be here

if not for

you.

    This also is a book for men. Brothers and other pants wearers who are too quick to dismiss women with brains, this book will serve as a prison release card. Too few men are able to unconditionally love a woman, or women smarter than they think they are. In an insightful and brilliant poem "Invisible Women" she speaks for the women world over, her sisters who are just trying to find their voices, seeking that which is most human and of necessity like an education or even more vital to healthy bones, love. She writes:

her first kiss is with bloodshed. she is a soldier for this. she was

just trying to find the love in it, like all girls do. searching for

god in a man, instead of her throat or heart. she wanted to feel

like a woman. whole, like her mother. who lives in fear. a fear she will

soon know as the way it simply is here. when you are invisible.

this is her body. she wanted to scream at 12. she is not ugly, she

repeated in the mirror at 14. she cannot stand up at 17. she is a

water sign with no water. their our thieves in her temple. there is no

fortress to protect her from herself. she is at the mercy of others.

being born girl is a sin, they say. bury it. hide it. burn it with

acid. give it no resources. this is a slow death.

Powerful words that also include, "this is your inheritance. keep it under your tongue. quietly. kenya. every 30 minutes. say a prayer. which? place this locket under your pillow. don't talk about the rape, huh?" In right questions begins the foundation for greatness or illusion. Rape can be physical and psychological, which ever or both do damage that may be beyond repair. It is clear to most honest observers that if any people withhold basic human rights to over one half of its population (women) that people are destined for failure. Look at Africa, India, Pakistan, Afghanistan, Mississippi, the Middle East and beyond. When will we grow up? If we truly love our mothers, grandmothers, aunts, sisters, wives, daughters, nieces, extended family women and truly care for the status of all women *God is Not An American* will help feed the positive yeses in our own presentations.

This stand tall poet is in the tradition of Gwendolyn Brooks, Zora Neale Hurston, Alice Walker, Barbara Ann Sizemore, Toni Morrison, Susan Taylor, Beverly Lomax, Toni Cade Bambara, Fannie Lou Hammer, Ella Baker, Carol D. Lee, Ruby Dee and thousands of un-named sisters who took the first step. We need to, as deeply as possible, understand the insides of Black women. How can we develop and ultimately free ourselves of this hidden weight if it is not recorded:

for every tongue we had to bite

for every heartbreak

for the dozens of times we've been called bitches

hoes, ugly, stupid, worthless.

for every jaw broke

every wrist cut, every pill swallowed.

every collect call we said yes to.

every bullet we swallowed.

in the name of love.

Often our greatest offense is silence. There is in most of us this "swelling in the throat" that seems to post stop signs in our minds, she has an answer in "adore me or die,"

it's only in pieces that we truly see how whole something was

how extremely perfect, when broken.

capturing the rush is the thrill

finding the space between

tear and floor

bone and skin

life and death

This is a book of tears, lost and found sons, betrayal, displaced memory, love notes, father songs, earth mamas, sculptured lines slowly building into stanzas, into poems, into a book that should be required reading in high schools, universities and from the pulpits of storefront and mega churches each Sunday.

Jessica Care Moore writes that "we don't claim that area of our beginning." Therein lies the ultimate confusion, without accurate history, without bonding traditions that do not go against progressive movement, there is no movement as in:

flowers, inside the dirt, digging through garbage, inside a smile,

behind a tear drop, inside the rainfall, between the hurricanes,

inside volcanoes, in the heart of storms, the ricochet of gunshots,

the abortion clinics, the after-hours, the pool halls, the lunchrooms,

the place between love and hate, under our noses, inside our books, our workshops, our classrooms, our elitism, our religions, our

politics, our individualism, our capitalism, our revolutionary songs.

There is a planting here as in vegetables; there are smiles and laughter in these pages. She is critical of herself as well as her people. This is not a woman's book; however I don't believe many men could have immersed themselves so effectively into the psychology of women or men. She, at times is quiet and contemplative and can be funny as all get out:

we may not always know how to swim

but we are not afraid of water

unless we're just leaving the hair salon.

Few brothers could have been so in tune with the complexity of hair days. She warns us that "a storm is coming," let me state in no uncertain terms, she is here!

Haki R. Madhubuti

Poet, founder and publisher of

Third World Press,

University Distinguished Professor and

Director of the MFA Program in Creative Writing at

Chicago State University

Dear Readers,

In 1996 I produced my play, The Revolutions in the Ladies Room at the Afrikan Poetry Theater in Queens, and later a longer run at The Nuyorican Poets Café. My good friends in life and in theater, Tureka Turk and Ka'ramuu Kush helped me to believe I could write beyond the page, and even put words in other people's mouths.

One of my heroes, John Henrik Clarke came out to see my play on opening night and afterward told me I sounded like Malcolm's. He was losing his sight then. I'll never forget that moment. I was still feeling my way through NYC, negotiating the new fame of It's Showtime At the Apollo and considering whether I would settle for a book deal or publish my book myself. I went on my first European tour in 1996 with Paul Beatty, (you must read his new book, *Slumberland*) whom i admired so much. I decided when I came home I would start Moore Black Press. Paul would tell me to make them call my appearances "readings" not performances. I understand what he was saying so much more over a decade later. I am a poet. A writer. I've never called myself a spoken word artist, but, yes I know how to read aloud! I tell young poets (especially black poets) the same thing now.

So many moments like these have inspired me in different ways, and have propelled my lifework and often pulled me all the way back to my beginning.

That's what this collection of poetry represents for me. This will be my first limited edition hardcover I've ever published. Our planet needs art and the work of artists when everything else has gone to hell. Even the poetic delivery of our new American President, Barack Obama, leans toward the artistic memory of this nation. I've never seen so many poets, singers, dancers, writers who wanted to be associated with an American President before.

Myself, included.

My book begins in Atlanta. Where I made my home from 2000-2007. Most of the work begins in 2004, when I am happily married to my husband Kenyatta Poole and I am a very hands on stepmom. Kenyatta had three wonderful children when we met, and I had an earth son, Omari, who I'd raised with his dad (my 1st husband, poet, Sharrif Simmons) till we parted ways in 2002. There are poems about the period I was not with Omari, that deal with the pain of his absence. Being an earthmom has been a big part of my life as a young woman. It is a love no one understands or truly respects unless they've done it. I'm happy to say that Omari has become a part of my life again and as I write this I am preparing to travel to Alabama to spend his 14th birthday with him.

Later in the book, the birth of my beautiful son, King Thomas James Moore Poole comes and so do more poems. I truly thought my life with my husband was just beginning, but I ended up choosing to leave Atlanta as the attacks on my spirit became to heavy for my heart and the safety of my newborn baby and my own well being were in question. The deep, *double betrayal* that occurs in my life becomes a turning point for my survival and my deeper search for my purpose, my spiritual foundation, my writing and most importantly my dedication to taking care of my precious new baby.

The first few days home in Detroit, I am booked to do a large reading at the Museum of African American History. How I was able to be in front of all those people without breaking down, I don't know. I left Detroit after my father died in 1994, and now I was returning home to find my footing again. I was still dealing with the heartbreak of my marriage falling apart, while trying to *negotiate* the sudden murder of one of my dearest friends of 17 years, Yale Guy Miller.

Detroit didn't feel the same without him in the city anymore.

After unloading a 24 ft. truck full of a portion of my life into a friend's garage, I fly out the next morning with King to the 2nd Anniversary of Hurricane Katrina, after a personal invitation from Susan Taylor. I am a shadow of myself, saying hello to friends/peers/activist, like, Mike Eric Dyson, Reverend Al Sharpton, Angie Stone and my first meeting with actor and activist Hil Harper who holds King during the candlelight vigil and allows him to tap on his nose while I sign a book for him. (Hil, you still owe King the signed copy of your book…smile).

The poem I wrote didn't come until I was caught in the rain with my son pushing his stroller near the Mississippi river in New Orleans. I wanted him to see the river. I ran to my room quickly, passing the lobby of cool people like Attallah Shabazz and Iyanla Vanzant. I had to write my poem, with my then nursing 1-year old son needing my attention and push out a poem that was not about my own personal tragedy. But something greater.

So, that's what God is Not an American is for me. It's my effort to continue to write relevant work to touch and heal people, strangers, fans, whomever, and still be able to give something back to myself. To have something left, despite any disappointments, because I know that I am living a blessed life. This is the 9th book from my press. A very precious number. My son was born on the 9th month on the 9th day at approximately 9pm. King's birthday is 9-9-09 this year. Poets Major Jackson and Sonia Sanchez both share the same birthday! (Yes, I was listening to Farrakhan break down the number "9" at the Million Man March).

So many moments pushed me to this place. What an accomplishment. To publish the wonderfully talented philanthropist, Danny Simmons, and his first beautiful collection of his deep, lyrical poetry and of course, his paintings. That book never received the attention it deserved. I love all the authors who've published through Moore Black Press: Saul Williams, Sharrif Simmons, Etan Thomas (yes, I do), asha bandele, ras baraka and Danny Simmons.

My life is so connected to the publishing work that I've done, and so I had to take a necessary step back to focus on my own writing. In the future, I hope to be an even smarter publisher. Outside of my family, Haki Madhubuti and Michael Simanga were two of the few people in the literary world who understood and extended financial help to me during my pregnancy. I hope to create future grants for mothers who are artists, or independent artist women who are expecting. Especially, single moms.
It is a delicate balance. An incredible gift.

This year I will direct a staged reading of my 1st play, at the Museum of African American History to coincide with a film screening of Ntozake Shange's monumental work, "For Colored Girls, "do a sold out concert with my new rock/soul/poetry band, The Detroit Butterfly Experience with my longtime friend Talib Kweli, premiere my multi media show *God is Not an American* at The Apollo Theater during their 75th Anniversary, and my son will play his first drumming gig with me. Detroit grounded me. The east wind is calling me. I will move fearlessly with my son.

2009.

The year of personal

change.

Love is Not the Enemy,

jessica Care moore
(one of God's favorite children)

God is Not an American
But God is definitely
smiling....

Letter to self: *(First)*
Atlanta, 2005

And so i need to write this book as i reminder to myself that i am a writer. Yes, i started this entry with an "and." walter mosley put a spell, maybe a root on me that i can't shake. i cry daily. While pretending to have it all together, and usually i do. the national black arts festival legacy panel was amazing this year, but that was the finished product. the stress of the weather and making sure everyone was on point, that's another story. i feel like a mama publisher. mama champ, the name the man in south africa gave me. there was tony medina and his tribute to michael jackson's skin. there was ras baraka, reading a poem he wrote that day about at the trial of the murderer who killed his sister. there was asha, in tears, reading her title poem that assures us that it is okay to be our own sexy dance partner, even in death or in a dream. etan, so humble, explains the importance of knowing who you are, and what type of human being you have to be if there are children who look to you for leadership and guidance. it was an awesome display. marcia jones, who painted three of our book covers, is working my book table, unacknowledged. she is beautiful and mystic. my husband is a film-maker today. i think he can do anything. i don't think i can.

I love publishing books. i just left the harlem book fair, my old neighborhood where poems jumped into my lap with ease. i couldn't resist reading a little piece of black statue of liberty. i miss it. it's too hot, at 94 degrees. only my husband and cousin lecca hold me down. a brown heavy set woman pushing a basket is talking to me from the side of the booth. i'm distracted by ras baraka who has that, "I might need to move my car," face. she is trying to explain, make me remember, how i met her at the apollo. i don't remember and because I am a shameless scorpio, i don't know how to fake it. i try to hear her, but there is too much going on at once. she didn't realize i had on my publisher costume and the wrapped skirted wonder woman poet lady was on a break for a few months. she is frustrated with me. i'm sure she thinks i'm a bitch. she smacks her teeth and walks away before i can turn back to her and try to remember. october 2005 will mark the 10th anniversary of my life changing appearance on it's showtime at the apollo. i can't believe people remember it or even care anymore. no pun intended. thankfully, their memory is better than my own when it comes to my own life. sometimes things, people, definitely places, are blurred together. my sense of time becomes more like my 5 1/2 year old stepson's. "i performed there yesterday," when it was really two months ago or last week. what is the difference, really?

Leave this to the ungifted. there has to be something other than ego in it. there has to be a gift to publishing. at least the publishing I do. what about haki? i understand his tears at furious flower more than ever. he is truly amazing. how do you find the balance? With love, with art, with work, with words? i am not certain i have found that place of peace. i know as i write this i am what i always am. tired. i haven't left my office in days. i've spent an extra thousand dollars on asha's book, just so she can have some during national black arts festival. A mistake has cost me an extra two weeks from the launch date. what can i do? ras' manuscript is finally being put in order on my mac. I love this book and i'm not going to rush it, i promise myself. The months fly by so fast. how am i to get this book to the printer and in the hands of whoever wants to read my stories, my poems, my jokes? Me and jomo* just cancelled our escape trip to paris. i think we will go to northern or western africa instead. sometime in october, maybe. I spoke with my cousin marvin today. his mom died. my sister lisa is in ohio with them. i wish i could be there. i miss them. i miss my daddy. the older you become, the more you realize it's all about where you came from. what got you to this place.

I have to stop writing. i think jomo may be taking me to dinner. Any place, but my office, in the basement of our beautiful new house.

*(*nickname of my then husband Kenyatta Poole—named for Jomo Kenyatta)*

sunflowers.
an opening prayer flower.

sunflowers. 2 dozen. growing slowly in my stomach. roots racing, traveling to the fire below. a brush fire. a burning bush. white at a funeral. the asian woman rubs my skin, says i look nice, then asks if i'm american. if i was born here. not by choice, i answer. not sure what i mean or if she understands.
"she says you are not black." says the voice shaving the stress off my feet with an illegal razor.

once i was mistaken for some kind of asian at a temp agency. my boss broke down and asked me one afternoon if i was "japanese or chinese."

i laughed and told her i was african. black daddy from alabama. white/non-american mother.

i was "let go" the next day.

could it be racism giving me those shooting pains against my ovaries a sharper edge. the stress from living in this country full of false patriotism. being black is not an excuse, but damn if it doesn't still make a difference.

the first of the month, i'm gonna send all of my stress related bills and health problems to george w.

today i watched some white haired evangelist using god's name in vain
to pray for a republican who doesn't believe in a woman's right over her own body.

whose god is watching this bizarre television show?

i think preachers should be banned from television.
at least in the middle of the night.
only nasty adult movies
six feet under reruns
and info-mericals after 2am!!

the devil does not have horns.
the devil has wire antennas.

baby come back to bed. it's 3am and yes, i want to just sit in the dark awake. no sound. no radiation comedy. no split screen life. just us, whole and quiet and young.

one day i'm gonna write some jazz poems. mari evans says she didn't
see the hip hop in me anyway. she is beautiful and brilliant and i
want to explain to her,

"that's what i've been trying to tell them all along."

you sound like us. she says.
of course. the music changes, but we don't.
we people of timeless discourse, blues blood
and passion pulse. this is how we survive.
old spirits carrying on in new bodies.

maybe this is madness and not a calling.
it depends on what you call madness
it depends on who's calling if i'm ever
home.
for some, i am forever missing.
for others, i am a moment away.

is there a such thing as choosing your
afterlife lover?
will you choose me?
who makes the final decision?
god, i would imagine.

who was the best to you?
who made you smile and considered your gentle heart.
scorpio and gentle do not fit in the same sentence.
only those who know you
know how tender your sting really is.

a sun petal is hot in your palms. no fear. pain is apart of life.
gather yourself up. love will never make sense on this planet. eat the
sun. borrow trees and stories. hide them where it hurts. bury your
worries in the deep of your womb. a treasure chest of doubt. you are
too young to be jaded this way. escape the light on your tongue. don't
chew with your mouth open. you can burn down a house with those
words.
your voice is a gift. loud on purpose. pretend to never know the
outcome.

love violently. but no matter what.

love.

amen.

a simpler god

when i was little

god

was not such a deep topic of debate.

god didn't separate our dinner table
or make us buy certain kinds of movies
or eat certain kinds of foods.

god was well. just god.

there was no any particular picture of god
in my house that i was told was god

so, we just assumed that meant
my daddy was god because
he had the biggest cadi, the loudest music
and like all good sheep

we were scared of him.

the older i get the more i realize
how important finding your god is very
important to other people.

it's like people i know are standing in these
god b-boy and girl stances..

(poses/movement/poses?)

and anytime there is a crisis in your life
they always say,

"well, i don't know what god you pray to…but.."

or eventually they just come out and ask:

"well what are you? who's your gang? your church
group? your religious righteous babe posse?

at some point you have to make a decision.

as al a am a lekem!!!
namaste

many of us forget
a ship named jesus
brought some of us over here.

lynching in the name of jesus
segregation in the name of jesus

a simple star in the heavens renamed
hundreds of times.
a rebellious disenfranchised
 jew of palestine

a brown man
a poor man
a revolutionary
a beautiful story
a poem passed down

a messiah
or maybe

simply the sun.

painted shadow
inspired by the lady who said i should consider botox

she died with no expression on her face
all her memories were kept in the heels of her shoes
her tears bottled inside of plastic containers
shipped to the local dollar store.
this was the water meant
to heal the world

smiles were carved inside her back
her true supporters knew she was happy
others who bathed or kissed her body
rumored to have heard her laughing

her life was a political existence
no ballot would elect her
no bullet would kill her
her existence was a narrow escape from death
a figment of some poets imagination
moments of surprise, came with no exclamation point
anger was a sedative for her pain
unnoticed, unchallenged
she won every bout she ever fought
laced up and painted red
her shadow was no match
for her skin and bones
and blood-dyed pink

she was called an artist
an interpretation of dreams
a spell-mixer with ink clots
that slowed her breathing
and toyed with her heart
so much was going on inside
her silhouette frozen in place
she died
no explanation or wrinkle
could be traced
she fell asleep forever
with no expression on her face.

the heart of a movement
(for elaine brown, juanita abernathy, evelyn lowery, and kathleen cleaver)

I wrote this poem for the *Atlanta Tribune*'s Women of The Civil Rights Movement Event in Atlanta at the Carter Center in 2003. I was still writing just a few hours before I arrived. I love this poem and the women it honors.

i bare witness
on this day
that all women are not created equal

i'm certain i would not be alive
if not for
you.

elaine brown.

not breathing and full of black power blood
lines tied to your birth.

it was your refusal to not let us forget about our
michael "little b" lewis
or other black magic children we pretend not to know
when we watch the paid off news
from our suburban homes.
the one's we forget to claim
after they've been drafted into the
prison industrial complex.
it's complex, to be a woman like you.
our minister of defense
battling for the
rights of women with your own comrades
in the movement
you taught us responsibility
gave us more than a taste of power
a lifetime of organizing and teaching
and loving and reminding the new generation that
we must talk and read about this country's history
simply because it exists
and wouldn't if not

for *you.*
and when they couldn't kill you
with church bombings where you taught
voter education classes

or with blasts through your living room
or daily threats against you and your families lives
your feet remained planted
when they walked in over 300 marches
when you discussed the possibility of dying
with your husband while you were still young.

juanita abernathy

we spoiled young women who speak
with the power of your tongue
we study with the blood of our elders on our books
and complain about the long walk to class
it seems that streets are not always named after
legends or mothers or survivors of a holocaust
for that matter.

when you are the wife of the reverend.
your life is a sermon
every sunday

a story of sacrifice and struggle
a vision of harriett retracing steps
of our journey
from selma to montgomery
in honor of sheroes
whose names would've never been known
sometimes it just takes one woman
to end apartheid
to build a monument
to stop toxic dumping into our backyards
you understood that the sclc was powerful
but sclc w.o.m.e.n was necessary
for our right of passage from girls
into law makers
you.
historical landmark

evelyn lowery

visionary
in our constant fight for
freedom

you.

one of our other mothers of
black art, black consciousness
you gave us the strength to take over
university presidents' offices
lay our bodies across basketball courts
to boycott racist newspapers
to demand classes closed on the
mlk holiday
to give african studies departments
professors with tenure.
you.
taught us education is frontline commitment
you.
woman of sncc.

freed huey
you.
woman of exile and love
you.

were never afraid of being radical
or becoming a full time student
of human rights
you.
sacred.
you.
not tired.
you.
destiny driven.
you.
kathleen cleaver
you.
evelyn lowery
you.
juanita abernathy
you.
elaine brown
you.
power seekers
you.
goddess
you.
sojourner
you.
you.

mariam makeba
you.
fire starter.
you.
nina simone
you.
international
you.
sister.
you.
mama africa
you.
truthteller.
you.
revolutionary
you.
woman.
woman.
woman.
you.
not still supposed to be here.
you.
not supposed to be here.
you.
bullet proof.
you.
panther.
you.
wife.
you.
breathing.
you.
bomb shelter
you.
ancestor
you.
pioneer
you.
frontline fatima
you.
half amazon, half amazing
you.
represent
the project monifa
the double-dutch champion

9

hopscotch heroin
voodoo candy lady
tree-limbed traffic stopper
the bubble gum popper
the pigtailed astronomer
everybody's baby mama
the storm calmer
a father's daughter
the birth of blues
queen of queens
you.
goddess
you.
warrior.
i am certain
none of us
would be here
if not for

you.

for my jomo

it's not that you put
rubies in my mouth
around my neck, or
on every finger.

it's the way my heart
beats faster
when you become the ruby
in my mouth, around my neck
and i
caaaaaan't

feeeeeel

my fingers.

honestly
for annie lenox

honestly, i cry too damn much. i try too hard. i fumble. i fail. i love again. i sleep between the sun and the moon. it's never enough. what i give is never enough. i want a baby. i'm still a baby. i wanna live on a star. you a rock and roll nigga. a south african butterfly. a tragic comedy of errors. i don't wanna do my hair. i'm broken in so many places. he feels wonderful. he kisses the hard spots. my shoulders are so small and strong. my music is teasing me. god is watching. i stand when i should sit. i laugh on beat. europe is not the world. open wide. can't protect the truth inside here. they will say you are white. white is not a color. connect the lines and destroy the dots. the clouds are indifferent to the ants below. this is shakespeare. this is the corner of harlem everyday. screaming is easy to ignore. i battle under my breath. on the page. whenever i am awake. honestly.

petition for a national holiday to honor the achievements of American women or Who in the hell else deserves a day off more than us?!

this poem is a petition
please sign, and move along.

columbus got one and macys has a
white sale. washington and all the u.s.
presidents, but not his african mistress,
not his black daughters

there's that one day they give thanks
for the genocide of native
americans
      and eat turkey

even jesus can't have his own day
he has to share it with some imaginary
fat man in a red suit who only visits the
rich annually

finally
and with much resistance they let
us have a day for martin but
even martin had help

if anybody deserves a day off
it's a black woman
i'm not talking about a day
that will shout us out
a token day of recognition
like secretary's day
(something cute to add to the calendar)

when i wake up on this morning on
    this day
i want some shit to
        shut down!
i don't want the mail to run
i want all the railroads to have a
moment of silence in honor of harriet
tubman. i want sojourner truth's name
to be written in swahili summer clouds
i want the original statue of liberty
to return back to her original african self.

i want stone monuments
for every rape
every daughter separated
& sold
for every child cut from her mother's womb
for every scar
the one's we can see
and the one's we push down
inside our stomachs, braid into our hair,
or spit down the toilet

i want a war memorial built off the potomac river
to represent the blood shed of the african holocaust
for the women who jumped off sides of ships
smothered their babies to save them
from a life of inhumanity

i want cynthia mckinney parkway in georgia
to be more than a green and white sign
i want to make this strip of highway
a better circle than 285.

this poem is for zora, coretta, angela, mary, mama stone
kathleen, rosa
vivian, irene, virginia, mama lovelady and every child
born girl
today.

i want sophia
the black goddess writer
who really wrote the matrix
to be given more than money
i want her to get the same all access keys
to all the studio doors
the wachowski wolves ran through with ease.
with her story in their teeth
and her womb in their pocket.

a black woman's life is a cheat sheet for humanity

i want octavia butler
to get a residual check on this day
for every sci fi movie ever made in the new millennium

i want my female classmates shot in the streets
of detroit to be memorialized and talked about
like the columbine students

for every black woman raising children alone
(any woman for that matter)
step moms, earth mommas, midwives, housewives
any woman who gave up her nine to five
and the one's who will never stop till they die or
retire.

i want the airlines to give them vouchers
so every black woman can touch the ocean on this day
can see apart of the world
they always dreamt of
something they created
but can't afford to enjoy

for every tongue we had to bite
for every heartbreak
for the dozens of times we've been called bitches
hoes, ugly, stupid, worthless.
for every jaw broke
every wrist cut, every pill swallowed.
every collect call we said yes to.
every bullet we swallowed.
in the name of love.

on this day this country will reflect
on the sacrifices of africa's daughters
who by force, have birthed your sons.

this is just the beginning of my demands

this poem is a petition for a national holiday
to acknowledge african-american women
for the systematic
use of our

backs.

tell me, will you sign up?

amazing walking foreign object

she was walking backward
down the sidewalk
past the funeral home with white horses and
black cadillacs to carry the dead.

she walked faster backward
than some could ever walk forward

her feet foreign, small
black satin asian-style slippers, black plants
yellow stained skin
finding an invisible line
on the concrete in southwest atlanta
for her feet to follow
to balance the unbalanced earth.

where is she going, i wondered?
this historical district surrounded at grease-point by
wendys, popeye's chicken and krispy kreme.

i followed her for minutes, then hours.
i stole magnolias from a nearby garden
and ran.
i lit candles and thought of her
before cooking dinner.

was she blessing us or preparing us?
i think of how times my past has crashed
head first into my future, sometimes
at full speed while standing still.

i step outside
balance my body above the ground on my lawn
i stare at the tree in front of my native blue and mauve house
i watch from broken blinds and shadowed sunlight
the elephant that hides in the bushes by my door listens to me type.
this is not action, this is writing.
when's the last time you really did a cartwheel, girl?

i don't fit on my block
the butterfly house, with squirrels living inside my roof.
the poet with different cars and sometimes children
blasting annie lenox, amel larrieux

and david ruffin
like he just dropped today.
don't u wish it would never stop raining?
don't u wish for 24 hour sunlight?

she's walking backward
in my direction in my head.
but i'm driving the wrong way

i crocheted her prayers inside
the fabric of every book i opened today
every eye wink met her face
and tickled her reflection

she cried for the faces of women
burned by acid or buried alive or thrown away
when born girl.

she cried for the black men and women
on death row.
she cried for the one's they let go
without resource
as an experiment
waiting for them to quickly return/back
                                    ward.

she cried for the bombs over harlem,
bombs over atlanta, bombs over detroit
bombs over iraq, bombs over dc, bombs
over brooklyn, bombs over chicago

she took me by my hypocrisy and kissed me
it was a backward kiss
upside down
a vertical language
un-foreign to my
french/arabic/portugese/amharic
mouth

it was a kiss of struggle.
a kiss that could stop a bomb
end a war. birth a nation.

she took my hand
warm and sweaty

held it tightly in a ball until i relaxed.

and we began to walk together for
blocks

undoing
all that man had
done.

written in a few minutes before heading to teach langston hughes
poetry workshop.

biology lesson
for omari

i sit inside my life as an observer
i boil tea and count the steps
i never noticed them before now.
next week they will be red and royal.
fat lipped for someone's feet to step on.

the wonder of poetry and explanation
politics and love seem so contrary
i rehearse a smile and leave for the panel
i entertain guests. i watch them watch me.
i listen to phone calls from friends who
never call to check for my heart.
everything is a lie. everything is the truth.

i bake his favorite macaroni and cheese.
i make his bed, purchase a twin
spiderman comforter with sheets and pillow cases.
they still smell new.

you love them and flop down and smile
when you come to visit.
there is no math, no parenting
just visit.
i'm unfamiliar with this song.
strange fruit. a mango in winter.
this was your house. our house.

your room.

some say i should make it my
workout center
meditation room
second office.

you want bunk beds for your 8th birthday.

i think about the bible story
i'm actually referring to the bible here.
the one about the two mothers
fighting over a child. a boy.
one mother who agrees to allow the boy
to be cut in two to please both sides.

the real mother walks away and decides
to allow the child his life
even if it is without her.
today i tried to do that with you
and i think you knew it.
on the upper west side
i actually tried to not call for the
third day in a row.
i was giving up. i was giving into a selfish world
doing what others told me to do

just let go.
just have your "own" children.
just stop loving your son.

you told me you loved me and missed me
over and over that day. promised to come
see me next month.
you wanted to know where i was
exactly!

i'm crying in starbucks on the upper west side
the *his/herstory film crew just called.
i'm at the wrong one.
how can there be so many coffee shops
on one new york block.
this entire city is sedated.

this is my life.

i think of us slow dancing in the kitchen
you falling asleep on my stomach.
your magnet science experiment winning first place.
you are all glitter and gold and "i'm fine mommy"
and missing.

you have been my reason for wanting to be
a better person, a responsible mother
a good parent, a teacher.

i never needed this country's courts
or legal documents
to love you.

i can't explain to you the madness of grown ups

why i wasn't invited for the holidays.
why you weren't reminded that it was my birthday
and now carry the guilt of missing it.
why we can't spend certain days together anymore.
why mommy can't do your homework with you
when she helped you learn to read and write and spell.
you had political artistic parents who talked about
the war, the government and all kinds of deep things.
but can't find a revolutionary way of loving you apart.
how will we divide the days?
the equation is complicated.
i hate math. i always will.

you remind me of all the times you would chase me
around the house with open jars of pickled herring

i am not a fish

but, you are my love child.

you make me laugh in places

i've never smiled.

five days out of the summer
august, 2005

somehow i am sadder while you are here
you asked me to put you to bed
i don't know how to react
you, long and lanky
tall as my chin
looking as if you want me to pick you up
and carry you to bed

i say okay
i cry in a corner.
i shake it off and kiss your head and cover you
with a blue satin comforter

i don't want to seem emotional around you
still, emotionless is not who or what we are

i see you bright fish, searching for the mommy
in me that is not gone
she seems reserved now. scared to love you
even as you lay on me and cover me up
while watching a movie on the couch.
you examine my fingernails
you have always been the one to take care of me

you like my husband and i'm glad

I am watching you become a man
i pray that you can see how much of my heart
you have taken up
how much truth i hold back
while i watch you sleep

when i don't write. i break.

when i don't write. i break.
glass. throw ceramics cups
into walls.
i crawl into tight spaces
i hide from myself.

how am I is supposed to grieve
the death of a child
that is not dead?

just missing from his room,
his bed. my life.

i don't know how to reprogram myself
into not being his mother anymore.

it is all i have known of motherhood.

i am introduced at his 10th birthday as jessica.
i have not missed one of his parties since 3.
i'm asked why i am late.
and i want to say,
"this time in this public space doesn't count."
i want to ask
"why haven't i seen my son in months?"

i say nothing.

i enjoy the private time we sneak on the roller-skating rink
we catch up on summer camp and how it feels to be 10
as we race in circles.
he says he feels different, and he is.

it is these smiles, and this moment, that is genuine.

i watch my husband offer everyone pitchers of coke
our 3-year old skates with a fearlessness
that is awesome and scary.
him and our 5-year old scorpion call the child i use to raise
their older brother.
they bring joy and family my life,
i will thank them when they are older.

tonight will be peaceful
i tell myself, crying, as we drive away.
depression is loud and ugly.
tonight i will gain control
have faith in the love from my first son
even as the moon comes down on this day.

for virginia woolfe

what will they say of a poet, woman
when she is gone?
her diary, a clock
for others to rewind
dissect us, lovers of language and history
tear us from our page

limb by limb

first take our lips,
then our tongues
comb our hair in place
and study our imperfections
until we are made perfect again.
since
you have nothing else
better

to do.

- at zen zero - lawrence, kansas

god is not an american

for nikky finney, jayne cortez, lucille clifton,
sonia sanchez and nikki giovanni

you don't have to be entered
to become a woman
in 1985 on a hot summer day in detroit
a group of us gathered
snotty-nosed underdeveloped hips
wet and wild lip gloss
john travolta and michael jackson posters
it was tea time
no, it was faygo red and half grown legs
crossing and truth or dare
we were 13
my dyslexic age now
full of cuss words and blue eye shadow
in black and white

okay, who is already a woman?
put your hands up
spread em…against the wall…
you have the right to be a virgin
lesbian, abstinent, female.

exactly what is the fee to be male?
just for a day – a hero –
for how much sex i've had before my
10th birthday.
bragging bout how i made one girl cry and told
her she was a baby because she was scared like a
little girl and i thought you said you were a woman
like your older sister?

does having your period count?
cause renee got her period and her breasts
when she was 11
so she wasn't scared of being a woman and showing off
her private to high school boys
in 11th grade i ruined my green and gold
basketball uniform so i could birth children one day
motherhood cannot be won
on a court
of backward laws

and fragile male egos
my jump shot is better now

at 13 i was scrawny and nappy
more interested in saving animals
then people or men
maybe i should return to my love
for dogs, birds and ladybugs
they didn't care if i was bleeding
or full of milk or sarcasm.
they knew i would protect them from
my brothers bb guns
my girlfriend sedricka was already doing it
to this cute boy clint - one of the few brown boys
at our catholic junior high school
everyone kissed clint or
mark, the white boy with large eyes
and long legs
 at least once

i think terrell was lynn's first.
wow, i have to call her and ask her.
i don't have her number in my head anymore
lynn.
my pretty play cousin/italian-french
sister who burped and listed to rock and roll
and fell in love with black boys.
she taught me about hair spray, homemade raviolis and
i admired her cross over and wished for her perfect teeth.
she was so confident in 7th grade
i thought she would be in movies or smoke
long sexy cigarettes.

there are long periods
sometimes they only last a week
the sound of women holding
their breath and tongues and screams
their whole lives
before realizing
all your childhood friends
the one's you trusted with your life
and keys to your diary
are gone

but this isn't a poem about blood or girlfriends or basketball

it's about being split open
in twos…threes…
crossing your legs and saying your grace
waving the right flag and shutting your mouth

god is not an american
no, god is not an american.
but she could be a woman
that would explain why we have sugarcane,
little red corvettes and chocolate.
and why she so graciously spared us an external sex organ
that would constantly get in the way of our brains
but maybe if women had penises
they wouldn't know how to cook, or wash or fix or kiss or blend,
or fold in all those special ingredients
that women bury inside the earth

and where do you think a woman would put her penis
during a time of war?

in the mouth of an intern?
deep into their father's history
pushing the same buttons
a decade later.

would she pull her penis out and begin
shooting at close range defenseless, poor children because
they have a different god with a different kind of penis all together?!

would this woman with the same destructive, big…
well, she thinks it's big anyway.
will she find a way to convince the world to build phallic replicas
of her bomb spitting penis in every major city.
would she enter little girls while they are still girls
cover their mouths and convince them this is the
"new normal."

when a woman is entered for the first time
no matter if she is a muslim, christian, or jew
third world or first world or end of the world
she has been conquered, deflowered and no matter
how many times i hear aretha and lauyrn promise
a rose is still a rose
i know there are more secrets
than this garden will allow.

a newspaper article reads: the terrorists
are wearing high heels
are they dr. scholls? nike?

i wonder if the high heel shoes worn
by a suicide bomber are made in the usa
or in a factory where child slave labor laws
don't exist for their exports.

so now i wear flat tennis shoes through security
because sometimes being a woman means saying no,
or refusing to garden, or cook or fuck or wear high heels
or paint toes and shave.

sometimes it's about cartwheels and chewing bubblegum
and being a daddy when there is no daddy or reading a book,
or burying your mother while you are still young
sometimes being a woman is simply about the mirror
about being alone
being fragile
cause breasts fall off and begin to sag and penises that once
entered you to declare you a woman
well, they lose their sergeant status
no matter how many wars they've started and innocent
people they've killed in their hard youth
they will one day have to face mothers.
brown black red and poor white mothers and explain.
what happened to our innocence
where is the rights of passage
the ritual, the beautiful secret
to becoming a woman?

is it bloody, is it forced, is it taken?
is it a lie, is it a story, is it a curse?
a war we didn't give birth to?
an apple we never picked.
how can we claim this child gone mad?
turning itself on it's own people.
a child disobeying his mother.

i realized early that black girls carry universes
inside their bodies
waiting to be named.

whole continents, land masses that were once connected

flow through her arms, fingers, chest, legs, stomach, feet
and head.
ghana is her heart her lungs cherokee her tongue
amharic her bones massai her breath aborigine her skin
the color of moroccan sand
and south african skylines
her blue blood
separates the atlantic from nile rivers and great lakes
the place where we shit and drink
the place where we love and hate
colonize and liberate
conquer and rebuild
rape and sew up
escape and imprison
the place where questions like
if you're a woman raise your hand
will get you killed.
the place where you enter and i exit
are not two separate locations
so please stop dropping contemporary bombs and
new school lies on my ancient and very wise pussy.

may 21, 2003@ 9:34pm

adore me or *die*

may 9, 2004 @ 2:27am

sometimes it is a swelling in the throat
an uneasy taking over in the heart
a pacing that is not easily hidden inside
of recipes or passed down secrets
it is just a sadness
a swiping sadness that fills up all that is empty
provides the blood to flow through my veins
and onto a sheet of white.

and what to paint, if not grief?
where else to write, but inside shadows
of what is really there.
still.
forbidden.
passionate, as a gunshot blast at close range.
it can blind you if you dare follow it's path.
it can leave you for dead.
this engaging of words and sounds and decadence
with windows you can't wait to smash
so you can see the reflection of life on the
other side.

it's only in pieces that we truly see how whole something was
how extremely perfect, when broken.
capturing the rush is the thrill
finding the space between
tear and floor
bone and skin
life and death.

a split second and it is gone forever.
the fate of one poem, lost in distraction.
untraceable   d n a
with no evidence of existence.
only what someone interpreted the moment to be.

it is this cycle that haunts the tired eye
the lover of night.

patience for her lover to appear
and disappear all at once
is the greatest discovery.

walking the line

he told me he liked my work
except that i was "walking the line."
what line?
the line you drew?
the crooked line. the bottom line is
you look nervous in holland, michigan

the tulip festival is in question
a bomb just dropped in the middle
of your pretty midwest garden
your comfort zone
under your ass just got hit!

you're looking for line breaks
when poems, cracked open
are the children of earthquakes

we have to write now because
when you're dead and famous
it's too late.
i don't want to be no postage stamp
i might mail myself to cote' d'ivoire
and never come back.

forgotten and buried alive in your
anthologies of anthologies
there are no lines of apologies
for the invisible generation
of black, latina, asian and native
writers you write off

as you cough and drink and lie
with your academic shields
protecting a craft you did not craft.

amiri said, it must be the witches
or maybe miles's bitches
your face turned blood red
as you stagger and grown green
from the line that separates me from you.

jess/ku (something smart ass, unlimited syllables)
black girl from detroit   5

31

can haiku better than you   7
classic? tell me who   5

how many white men can wear
one shoe?

handicap by design.
you never in the tradition of being you
you hop around the page
trying to deconstruct what i do
i'm walking the line.
the picket line.
the welfare line.
the grocery stores lines.
the reparations line.
oh, they forgot to make that line.

people like order. structure
the prison line up.
the long club lines.
stay in line. know your line.
get out of that line.
the never ending lines that count time.
and forget to tell the line keepers
you were born, you wrote books, shut
universities down when necessary, produced plays,
scored films, danced like a gazelle, sung like a
freedom march, loved when on one else loved back,
buried our young, passed down our stories, composed music,
evaluated, excavated, deconstructed, and even prayed.
did we pray? we boycotted. we bled. we were born
inside a line that is continuous, ancestral pull
a tradition built with brick and bone and steel
love, revolution and will

this is, afterall, the only mutha fuckin
line we got.

a line i dare you to walk over
a line sometimes too unbearable for breath

a line i am attempting to walk
despite the amputation of my legs
and the fear in your voice.

nina

for umi and the movie that i can't wait to see

like the gun. like my blues. i don't have no love for you. born into darkness. i fascinate the light. smoke to escape. black eagle in flight. nobody gonna love you like i do/i got wings and long legs/i'm the scarface barbie toy with no adjustable parts/toes come painted/ statements, blanket/no shelter/no glass house/turquoise lips lined in gas/catch my mouth on fire/with one long match/boxing with your shadow/a ghost of my own past/and you won't last a block/a week/ lifetimes times lifetimes/shotgun on my porch/old south/new north/ same system/cotton mouth/cotton clothes/i don't love these holes/41/ my body can't take no more/i'm sexy on the trigger/most wanted/pretty nigga/turbulent times/my momma's pain/indifferent ocean/wash my hair/dressed in pink/i'm a gangsta baby/and my shit don't stink

About being a poet

may 5, 2007

tonight i cried about being a poet.
strange to cry over such a silly thing
i read two interviews with two women

poets
lucille clifton and suheir hammad

then i cried.   because they reminded me
that i am still a poet
even when i haven't written a poem in months
not one that i would read or publish

because my 8 month old son
just climbed the entire length of our staircase
and this fascinates and excites me so much i don't have
time to take a picture of the moment
let alone write a poem about it

and who would want to hear a poem
about the domesticated mommy jessica?

who spends her days balancing her baby boy
on her lap   while checking emails and imagining her studio time
while publishing other people's poems
trying to convince local poets that i have
not evaporated into i-20
moved back to new york city
or hate the poetry scene.
(well, maybe a little of that.)
instead i've committed myself to nursing
my son for at least the first 12 months of his life.
and when i do have a "break out" and show my face at
night. it usually ends with my breasts engorged
and me running to get to my child to suck me back
to mommy normal.

so, most nights it's just easier to run
my company. focus on my writing when i can.
polish up a few old poems. work on a new play.
while flipping through baby einsten and zen baby dvd's
flashing back to that great
tribute to betty davis   ryan waters on guitar

variety playhouse
i was skinny enough purple
short body suit red blow out afro and pink hooker boots

i was born with it
i will die with it
because it's in my blood

black women rock

imani uzuri divinity and tamar kali
that beautiful show a different kind of me produced
in atlanta. a southern city i still haven't set my foot in.

after nearly 7 years.

as a scorpion, i am mortified by that great number
how could i possibly be in one place this long??

how can i be reduced to crying over being
who i am
no matter how displaced this art form can
sometimes seem
and no matter how many international shows i do
i am still the poet from the apollo. a police officer in the cnn
building recognized me today. didn't he see my invisible costume?

you are right suheir
we should not have to always be ready to read a poem
on sight
or be anything other than women on
any given sunday
we must only be human.

today is my first birth mothers day
people who know me know i'm sensitive about this day.
i've had so many nice mothers day with omari
he is 12 and i haven't seen him since 11
the first full year of his life i've missed and it hurts.

only one of my step children called me today.

i remember my step daughter kelsey telling me
she thought of me on mothers day and wanted to call me.

that was all i needed, i told her. just the thought.

still

today i am happy with being the
queen of king's universe.
my son who doesn't require a permission slip
from anyone else to freely love me.

i know my beginning.
my roots are books and i think books are
sexy. my music is stevie and smokey and marvin
rolling stones and teena. my heart is my daddy's
my husband's
my children.
my poems.
i don't know as many by heart anymore.

i think i can still be a rock star poet
while holding a piece of paper in my left
the mic in my right.

it's 12:27 and it feels like 4am.
i've been up since sunrise and i am sneaking
to type this poem quietly next to king
who is teething & uncomfortable.

growing pains never stop baby
we only find new metaphors to cover it up
relocate yesterday's tears inside tomorrow's poems
and continue to write.

there are no poems

there are no poems
in sushi bars
or haughty fifth avenue boutiques

most poems have

bled
slipped on concrete
out ran a bullet
stolen something
loved violently
and smiled   at the devil
at least once.

all poems are addicted to something
someone.
all poems have
lost
cried
considered death
at least once.

there are no poems in sushi bars
or expensive fifth avenue boutiques
at least not the kind of poetry
that would ever belong to me.

not your average angry black woman poem

i don't know who hurt me first
in which direction i was looking when the first
sucker punch found it's way to my cheek

but as i look into his face
beat down today from past scars

i am certain.
i am a woman scorned.

and even though i hate the way
black men label
black woman poets as
angry
man-hating
lipstick lesbians
who don't need a man

today
i am using this moment
for a sense of clarity

because the only black men
that i've loved
who have not at some point

cheated
lied
betrayed
used or
fronted on me

are men who look only like
my daddy and my brothers

and i don't mean brothers
in the conscious, african-centered
way
or the boys you love
when there is no intimacy
because they have broken my
unromantic heart as well

i mean, jonny and mark
ed, billy and william

moore

maybe it was michael wroblewski
the white-bow legged boy
with the scratchy voice
i secretly found cute
in 3rd grade
who ruined me first.

or maybe it was my friend roderick
the only black boy who
went to my school
who lived on my block.

the one who told me to come
behind his house and proceeded
to show me his pee pee.

but i was grown by then
at least 10, anyway.

or maybe it was my brothers'
friends mark or orlando
who made me turn bright red
when they would smile at me.

or joseph
whose house i couldn't pass
if he was sitting on the porch.

or rico
my play cousin who i watched
all my friends fall in puppy love
with
and i became his sister.

i adored black men from the first
time i ever left out my house
so, i thought they were all sent to earth to
protect me.
love me.
show me how to play basketball.
buy me ice cream.
beat up anyone who messed with me.
worship me..
sing me songs in david ruffin voice
with temptations steps.

there was a time i would hand a man
my heart and ask him to keep it

in his pocket
until i needed it back.

so am i wrong to write
that along the way
you all ruined me a little bit

before i became a revolutionary
before i forgave you
i made excuses.

it was the white man.
it was slavery
america's oppression
willie lynch

all the reasons why

i always lock my car doors
and put up walls that never used to exist

you owe my husband an apology
(*and now he owes me one*)

from my first kiss

to my prom date

the first one i literally
caught in the act of cheating.

and for the first gun to my head

the light skinned guy i met on new years day
in 1993
who i always thought was bad luck
because my daddy died the next morning.

all my new york mistakes
and those who aren't worth naming
even in an abstract way.

you are the reason why
i love with fear.
that i am always waiting
for the fairy tale
to turn into
a nightmare
no matter how perfect it feels
or how much he reassures me how

much he loves me.

i have been forever traumatized

like any girls who's ever cried
when they realize it was just
sex for him

or

that your time was
just the most convenient

or

maybe he just needed a
highly decorated
babysitter

?

it took me 31 years to find
a love that would force me
to face the demons of my past.

my jomo aggressively loving me to the point
that i was taken off guard.
i brought out my sun tsu.
i couldn't take a compliment
or an honest "i love you,"
without wondering what was going to
hit me as soon as i let my guard down
or god forbid
i actually loved him back.

and that's not a woman
who hasn't loved, given, sacrificed,
stayed up late praying
fought other girls in your honor…

and despite pretty girls smiling in my direction
i never trusted women enough to get down
which is probably a whole other poem

so, i think i have the right to say

that there was a time when i
would've jumped in front of bullets
given you the keys to my car, my house
my bank account information

and you took a little bit of that away

i wasn't an americanized black girl
who demanded you have a 401k and
a lexus

i loved you for just being.
for surviving.

for looking like my daddy and my brothers
men who never violated me or hurt me

who am i to blame if not you and you and you?

what have you left me to say to my sons
about the little girl in their class
they fall in love with

when she is guarded

or

when her kiss trembles

or

she cries for no reason

or

when he marries her and

sometimes she doesn't trust you
when you come home with flowers
or tell her you love her daily

and who else do i have left to thank
besides
my daddy and my brothers

and the beautiful circle of male
friends i've kept close…

for having something else besides
pain to pass down
and more than
angry black woman

poems

to write.

a series of mondays
(2004-2007)

i was searching for a poem i'd just begun writing in 2007 called monday and then i found this…something i wrote in 2004…wow. it's such a sad piece, but i like it. i think i'll add it to the monday poem i've been writing in my head for these last few difficult months of my life.

monday, april, 2004

the mornings are blue and orange. i can't offer much to the sun today. i pray and try to sit lotus in the middle of a one way street. watch the birds for a sign. red tails. beautifully dipped feather brushes. i paint the invisible line of my body. there is no proof of bruises, but they are everywhere. below my eyes. near my heart. dancing around my ankles.

i smile at the neighbors. i am screaming at the top of my lungs. i am on fire, walking toward the park. i burn no one. i escape into the bag in my hand. brown paper in my brown hands. crumpled and light. jagged edge. i sit below a tree with carvings on its skin. a scroll of bark filled with words, a silent prayer scratching at my back.

monday, december 31, 2005

i am drinking red zinger
tripping over my plans
already

moore black press made
the "power list."
a friend calls to tell me

i've been thinking of
walter mosley lately

i know i must write
and write again

but i must find a way to
continue to publish

etan two-ways me jokingly

remember me?

more than an athlete.

of course, i do.

2005 was my big publishing year.

etan, asha and ras next week.

danny simmons will be a break-through
table top book

i am a poet and i want to call haki
to ask him how to keep up with

being a poet

or writer
with a major book deal

poets that live off their parents
and now

i'm wondering where is the grant money
for a woman poet who has made a
living writing and reading poems
for 10 years

now that she is pregnant.

i am already a mother

i remind a guest in my house
days before.

i already raised and loved my oldest son
who turns 11 this year.

me and my husband already have
two boys and a girl we love

i am already a mother

this was supposed to be
my "rock star" year.

drop the third book,
god is not an american
and finish a music album.
finally do some work with spike lee
turn my books into theater shows
(i have to remember to call reg e)
do the feature role in nzinga's romantic comedy

january 3, 2006

my daddy died 12 years ago today

death is always waiting for me
every new years eve
but this year
for the first time
i enter with life

and life is scary and fragile and beautiful

and it's the first time in years
i thought about doing something else

as much as i love poetry
and have enjoyed publishing

i'm already booked for a panel in london
a performance in toronto this fall

i keep hearing a voice whisper/yell

jessica you have to be still
you can't be flying all over the country
you're going to have to wait on that
international trip we were planning

jessica, you have to be still

i know you don't know how to do that
but, you have to learn

you have to write about being still
the revolution will have to wait
while a revolution
inside you
grows.

monday, march 12, 2007

happy birthday daddy. this is such a hard day for me every year. i miss you so so much. i wish you could see your grandson. the first of irene's clan. i wish you were here. my life would be so different. you always took care of me, treasured me. i've never found a man who loved me that way. only now, with my son king thomas…i knew i would name my first son after you…do i see love like that.

maybe i'm not meant for "romantic" love. it never seems to work for me. you were such an important part of my life. i never imagined you not being here. when i go through a hard time as a woman, i wonder how much you could help me get past it. i know you are my angel. i'm asking you to please look after me, look after my son king. please ask god to protect us. remember my friend yale? someone killed him. it's the worst feeling since i lost you. yale was always good to me...probably because we were just friends.

Monday, July 7, 2007

today is not a day of prayer
no forced barbeques and fireworks
without freedom
this summer
everyday was an endless stream of
Mondays

i stopped watching the news for a few months
i ignored my broken cell phone
just to see what would happen

a terrorist attack
a European child gone missing
a riot on bill maher
a cure for aids
an end to the murder in darfur

anything

i am happy and sad all at once
in a split second anything can change
these days.

tears invade my joy
a snake-skinned shoe
disguised as friend tries to
get in the way of my journey

my friend angela has wrapped her angels
around us courtesy of jesus
dawn is a tree of wisdom

i hear allah in my son's mouth

the devil is a lie, i am promised.

i am only a fountain
waiting for my husband
to find me.

again.

at 15 months.
for mothers

your first real steps
you gave me as a birthday gift

you must have known how much
i needed you to grow up a little faster
than average babies.

you wiped my tears
when you were just learning what tears meant

but somehow you could tell mommy
was sad
and this made you silent
& i could see the man in you
at just 10 months old

you must have known my heart was
broken. since that is the place
i kept you my whole life.

i prayed for a son i could show
the world too again. who i could
teach to read and crack jokes with.

a baby i could take to my shows and
watch grow into his own kind of poet
or drummer or gymnast or scholar or

whatever he dreamt up in his own head.

and no one could ever take you away from me.

and unless you've loved a child
that is suddenly taken out of your life
& there is nothing you can do about it.

no magic. no poem. no court of law.
that will help you.

then you may not understand.

i have been a mother for over a decade
people who really know me, know that.

but king thomas made me official
in this society of neglected
motherless and fatherless children

we the people
full of god complexes
and hypocrisy

it takes more than 10 months
to be a parent.

and i'm still trying to figure out

why the most beautiful
and talented people i know
are still the one's with the
least amount of money?

finding daddy's grave
pension row. madison, alabama.

the place i was born
everybody's daddy was/is from alabama.
they wear hard hats to work
in the morning.
and wipe their red clay at the door
every evening.
their construction is molded
in southern geography
and buried beneath the surface of
northern skin.

we don't claim that area of our beginning.
we ain't from down there no more.
up here we underestimate the strength of silence
the value in growing your own greens, tomatoes and okra
in our own backyard.
being humble, saying hello and knowing who lives
on the corner house and the one
`round the block
behind the old park
right next to that new highway
          we pretend we didn't see
          the government quickly build.

we can only see what used to be

breathing
          there.

and so we refuse to drive on top of it
in quiet protest
because we might run into those pecan trees
or aunt maddy's aloe vera healing garden.

in the future court of supreme
there will be old women drapped in black robes
suspended in midair
with fresh tomatoes growing from their ears
ancient medicine pouring from their tongues
and no physical proof that our ancestors
used to live in a house
right below this land
way back in 2005.

forgotten crimson rivers
pour out when we cut ourselves
we just apply a bandaid
continue in our position as new negro.
we had to swim hard
to get to the luxury of
our upscale, modern, art deco
freedom
but, freedom from what?

when i lost my daddy for the first time
in 1994.
i found my south mouth
alabama tied tongue
rattle snake conjuring word magic
hiding in my gut
translated through my aunt susie,
cousin dukie, aunt jessie and annie mae

"you are all of them girl. look at you. definitely t.d.'s daughter."

i found poems that didn't always apply to my own life
and information i hadn't read in any school books
while i was "getting my lesson."

since his death i have traveled to south africa, germany,
scotland, england, holland, france
and all over this country.
but it took me 11 years to return to a small
town named   madison.

wearing inappropriate pink slip-ons, white pants, tattooed skin and
hair wild and thick.
i traced the bricks, rocks and whiskey laced foundation
of pension row

t.d.'s place.
built with his own hands in 1946.
a historical landmark with broken windows.
sacred ground
where his war money was hidden in jars
sponsoring other black boys
to move up north to detroit
to find work and assembly line salvation.

a southern funeral is not a corporate, tailored
pretty event.

wigs fall off.
jesus comes.
the holy ghost makes everybody dance funny.

i was 4, maybe 5 when i saw my first dead body.
my uncle columbus was light, almost white
looking back at me with closed black eyes and hair.
i watched them lay the dirt on top of him.
i wanted to know why they were putting him in the ground.
i wanted to touch him. ask him how it felt.
i asked white people i saw
if they were gonna vote for
george wallace
in my best fake
southern accent.

southerners understand superstition
so when thomas moore left the earth
i knew i'd have to see him properly
settled in this red unfamiliar ground
with my own eyes.

after living the last half of his life in the motor city
he insisted to be buried in a plot of dirt
already assigned and paid
for down south.

at 22, it was the first time i flew
anywhere with my daddy.
a claim check for his casket
floating through the sky.

this time there were no stops to
chattanooga's look out mountain
no green ragtop cadillac
blasting gladys knight
the quick flight
avoids the short cuts
and the branches of cotton
we'd pick along the drive

like most of the black north
we like to fly over
our past
at full speed.

fathers day, 2005

i drove from my new home in georgia.
finding my daddy's grave became a journey
into his life.
it had been 11 years and if i wanted to find
the correct madison cemetery
i would have to first find my cousins
and listen to them remind me of who i was.
learn "how my daddy never cussed or drank or anything."
i silently laugh and think about my mother
and their loud fights
& southern comfort bottles near his bed.

i try not giving away
my inherited big weak teeth.

we pretend to understand the directions and head
"toward the carwash
across from the antique store
near the big street."

we know we are lost as soon as we pull off.

we stop at the first cemetery
fighting the sunset.
husband and sons take the front entrance area
our 4-year old detective screams, "i found it," at least three times.
"i see an m," says 5-year old jaden, who like me,
doesn't like graveyards, but is trying to help anyway.

we walk over other people's fathers, children, mothers,
grandparents and wonder who they are.
some of the tombstones are magnificent shrines.

waterfalls and fresh flowers

we find out later this is the "white"
segregated cemetery.

we travel across the street to a darker, poorer lot of land
with scattered bodies.
night is coming and i am overcome with grief and shame.

i can't find my daddy
and it's my fault.
my legs are weak and my stomach is sick.

i am native and foreign
my cherokee feathers have forgotten
                their way

i buried the south
put it in my mouth
and swallowed my own geography.

how can you forget directions to a place
that lives inside your stomach?

"let's just go."

i try to call for my husband while he is
on the cell phone with my brother jonny
asking him to describe the flat, simple government issued name plate

they give veterans.

i think about how revolutionary it was for my
daddy to insist on being buried here.
how everyone thought it was inconvenient
i decide at that moment
when i die
i will be buried right next to him
my heart in the mud of madison
so my kids will have to travel.
be uncomfortable
search
face themselves.
claim their past
when they come to lay flowers in my memory.
when they "pay respect" it will not be
just for me.
i will ask them to wipe
blood red mud on their foreheads
and cheeks

I will leave them signs in the trees
markings in the grass

and a mirror.

Half American
for my mum.

I never really got you
Non-American woman
Alien to loud boom box music
You were an Anne Murray
And Barbara Streisand fan
Reserved and sometimes british
Always putting milk in our tea
What were you doing in segregated
Detroit?

Pushing out yellow black boys and then
Me. Your reflection that would fight you back
Maybe you had my sister
Because you knew something more
Gentle and girl
Was inside of you.

It couldn't just end with this scorpion double-tongued
Fire-child
With thick ponytails
And more mouth
Than a Cadillac muffler
But, I made you laugh
Even though you would cover your face
I could see you.
Curious creature that you were

It wasn't until my daddy died
That I really wondered who you were
This brown-haired lady who I lived
In the same house with most of my life.

I wonder how you, Canadian and proper
Ever saw yourself living the rest of your life in
This Chocolate French city full of removed
Southern Africans.

Giving birth to children
And this girl

Who would challenge you.
Debate your politics

It was your silence that scared me.
I knew there was more going on inside your house
Your body and I never understood why you didn't
Scream!!!
And when you did finally feel fed-up, unloved, confused,
Displaced.
Why you sometimes thought I could handle your anger
I was your strong oldest girl
Your prosecutor and your best defense.

Still
You are the reason why I know all the songs
On the soft rock station
Why I still need milk in my black tea
While you have turned to coffee.

You are the only person
I trust with real tears
And without words or music or
Affectionate hugs
(you know how the English are about
showing emotion.)

I know you love me
Because you allowed me
To be myself even if you didn't "get it"
At first.
My nationalism, my love for Islam and Malcolm
Years later
You consider applying for your U.S. passport
And I want to tell you "No!"
Don't do it. You vowed after the sixties riots
And the assassinations of Martin, Malcolm and Kennedy
to never become a
Citizen of this country.
As I listen to your helpless complaints about the president
And local government.
 I assure today there are even more reasons for you to
Keep your silent protest alive.
Maybe it's just for me.
You are the reason I understand the beauty of
Cooking for someone you love
And the great pride I have
In only being
Half American!

competitive eating

i listened to sometimes democratic senator lieberman say it was about time they started "randomly stopping and searching people on the trains," especially those with backpacks.

in new york city, the people who carry backpacks are:

hip hop heads who need to carry several of their favorite cd's and headphones. mothers carrying babybottles, coloring books, crayons, ziplock bags full of pretzels, hi c drink boxes, and granola bars for the long ride to the bronx. women, with one or more children who need the use of their hands to hold other hands. students, who must carry books, rulers, notebooks, phone numbers and sometimes an extra change of shoes and clothes for gym class.

the new paul beatty book, *slumberland*, ray stone's *eat like you give a damn*, some extra bags of earl grey tea, my mac, coffee flavored lip gloss, black bic pens, asha's new memoir, a french-english dictionary, a picture of king, a man i love, a travel scrabble game, and a small piece of chocolate mixed with lavender.

not terrorists.

flying high on love/pray mama
14 fevrier, 2004

it seems i am always
praying in the sky
maybe because i feel
closer to god when
death is close.

or maybe the angels, cloud spirits
and water mermaids
enjoy dancing past my eyes
centuries old

my young nerves abandoned
inside a sun i used to worship
at 11, i would've loved to
have the chance to be this close

i am forever with child
like everyone with seeds, dirt, hands
a thousand wolves surround my womb
bonfire for the unborn/born
fire-child with freckled face
often terrorized by life
afraid to breathe
today red and white carnations
in my hair
disguised as bookmark

she wears a heart
where i wear a plastic rose
we are not lovers/we are women
shaking in the discomfort
of our skin
brown, black, and pale walls
with oval windows
closed shades & battered light
who will hear our screams for mercy?
our twilight prayers
shooting pains of needle
inside our knees
attempting to move in a space
that won't ever bend

my stomach turns in circles
i wait to kiss the ground
to walk on hot coals
barefoot and pregnant

flying is so over-rated
praying is necessary
birth is the only thing
that makes sense

So, what are you gonna call him?
for my first born son king

if you are going to push him out
right here in the middle of the
right wing reign
despite the wars like wild fires
and democracy   never

if you are going to open your legs
in the middle of mine fields
while bombs hidden inside
of free bowls of rice
blow
death winds
crying out in the night
stealing our children with rhythmic breath
and no drums for music since the
integration experiment
failed

if you're going to cry freedom
wear black in october
and paint your mailbox red
to keep the colder-sack alert
then why wouldn't you name him

king?

when you have spent the last decade
in an undeclared state of war
against nine to fives
and slave labor
and begging for vacation time
and kissing ass

why wouldn't you?
when 1 in 3 are headed to
privatized prisons
and living past 30 is unique
unharmed and without record
is unheard of

you actually know his daddy

you even married him!

if you're gonna raise him
as something greater than
what this country has promised
a survivor filled with the blood
of royalty
a lion father and poet for mother
if you have the will to somehow
still believe in black love
get married in red and dance to
slow jams
in the middle of the day

if 4 year old israel calls his name
during a libation the day before
new years eve

what do you suggest we do?

ignore the ancestors?

what would make you more comfortable?

young white female nurse at
northside hospital.
working inside a institution that delivers the most babies
in the country.

who told me
"we never heard of anything like
that before."

while removing my stiches.

who is this we?

the committee of snotty nose white girl nurses
or the pharmaceutical companies
who make a living off our addictions
to their legal drugs
over the counter promises
or the epidural doctors
who get paid to play catch

my rosemary, echinacea and aloe ancient
natural healing remedies
make you nervous
you feel uneasy and unnecessary

nurse ruth

why do you want him sedated and sleepy
what is wrong with a black man born
awake

proudly named.

i know the nappy corned rolled hair is misleading
but i am not an uninformed 17 year old unsure of who my
baby daddy is.
and suddenly i realize exactly where i am.
my blackness laid flat against paper white sheets
my personal anesthesiologist waiting in the wings

so, yes, you will read my signs we taped to the door
of what not to do to my son
and if i need something to kill the pain
worse then your racism
you will address my husband

stop talking to me
and leave my room.

this is said while gently applying pressure
to her wrist

if you say you fight against imperialism
and believe in economic freedom for the poor
if you are tired of black men being raised
without fathers
or by americanized culturally inept mothers
who teach their sons to love money,
hate their fathers, and only
pray they make it to the nba or nfl or
become a famous rapper one day!

if you're going to attempt to birth a nation
of loud, beautiful mutha fuckas
who love themselves, love art, love music,

love their women, their culture, their mothers,
their family, each other and yes,

even love his own name

King Thomas James Moore Poole

when people asked me
what i was going to call you

after i told them your name

i responded with this poem

and this promise.

it's what they won't ever call you

that matters.

Jupiter

After being asked why I write about so much
about oppression in my country.

when i go to jupiter.
i'm gonna write some jupiter poems
but i live here

mutha fucka.

so that's why all these poems
are all about
you and

this place called America.

"God is closest to those with broken hearts."

—jewish proverb

When the Little Brown Girl Gets the Holy Ghost

(or the baby Jesus story revisited)

I am probably pregnant at this moment
with a savior
I got at least a few hundred names of
Potential Mary's
in my cell phone on speed dial.

Imagine it must be hard to deal with
Having a child alone.
Especially one so anointed.

Many of us have imagined our own Joseph.

Fine, tall dark man with stars in his eyes
Mouth singing Marvin Gaye songs
Or playing with John Legend or Marc Cary
                                        Piano/keys
A man with carpenter hands
opening the doors of our homes.
Before we walk inside at night.

A man with the moon in his pocket
And kisses like childhood chocolates
A man who walks in a room and examines
The way the wood floors are laid.
Thinks he can do it better, if you ever was looking
To upgrade the room. That is.

Joseph who clears your walkway to insure
the fall leaves don't
Ever touch your winter toes.

He doesn't even care if he was the big winner.
He's gonna love anything growing
Inside you.

Girl.

That's God's work. Gotta respect that.

Right?

Yes. I understand the need for this story

More than ever now.

I don't know a woman more lonely and outside
Of the world then

A pregnant one
who's baby daddy is a mystery.
Or maybe he's just in denial/river.

Still, there was no mystery to that swimming
Contest that   guppy knew exactly
where he was

When he hit the finish line.

Can almost mark the date in December.
They love thinking they chose it, you know. The very moment
It goes down. Classic comedy. Just best to laugh
Under your breath and share the joke in private with the
Growing seed.

That's when we start talking to ourselves with
No apology.
This is when God is close and the extra heart beat
Keeps us hungry for strange things.

Full sweet watermelons. pralines and cream
            and jello.

They love us. Best sex, some say.
Funny how the most thug type of man
Will tell you how he's scared to hurt that baby

Jesus!

How many mangers, hallways, hospital rooms,
Bathtubs have been the home to births

With no men present ??

Just a woman pushing and praying and turning
Purple and green and orange
An exorcism of every small pain she ever felt
Every lover that passed through
Smells of Hennessey and short breath and

Sometimes there is cocoa mango
Mixed with black and milds
Frankincense & Myrrh
ain' t always
Readily available for the holiest of
Holy births.

They made a patch to try to stop the
Goddesses from producing so much.

We making too many girls they say.
Man's small world ain't right with the imbalance.
How's a man gonna pick just one?

How many modern day Joseph's turn Judas
On their Jesus?

How man modern day Joseph's have turn Judas
On their baby Jesus?

Their sons and daughters
with their blue blood dancing through their veins
Their hard laugh and their unexplainable sense
Of music at two years old?

Who am I, If not a forced Mary?
The Black Madonna with a baby stroller
And not enough hands or time to manage
This unnatural phenomenon
Called single   motherhood.

A woman with the love of God growing in her belly
And the only father he knows is the one she prays to.
Cause the one in the picture on the dresser
only calls once in a while.
Just to hear the sound
Of my voice.
or to see if he can
still make me cry.

Three wise men are simply not enough.
Bearing gifts at abandoned births like these.

So I left
a full plate of chocolates and melons and rum

near the river I prayed to that ran behind my home in
Georgia

& Yemaya
answered.

So I named him King of the babies.
The light of my world.

These sons will have mothers
Who will have to learn to be fathers.

Rosaries will carry prayers in her name
Some religions will erect statues
Even worship
The miracle of this type of birth

Don't we deserve so much more
Than basic child support?

With a son of God
drinking life from
our bodies.

Didn't you say you were A God

Son?

Weren't those your words?
That your blood line was revolutionary
And (Malcolm) Little and (Elijah) Poole's of blood
Ran through your veins.

Does that make u some kind of Muslim?
I actually used to see Malcolm in your face.
Until I realized I was really just Betty
In search of her reflection.

John Henrik Clarke told me I sounded like
Malcolm.
He'd lost most of his sight, but
Came to see my first play.

Maybe I was Detroit Red after all, not you.
Maybe I should start listening to the almost blind

Cause sometimes the most visionary of men
Are just turncoat griots.

Cause when the little brown girl
Gets the holy ghost

I said.

When the little brown girl gets the holy ghost
And it's not one cue. Or planned
And she hasn't been to a good Baptist
Church in years.

She can recite Surahs and Psalms
In the same breath.

Cook poems and write dinner
Change the world and diapers
With her left hand.

Rock a mic with her right.

And pray that one day her own baby Jesus
Will be able to exchange the heavens
For a mirror and see himself as the greatest
Reflection of

God.

after speaking of loss
for lucille clifton

i began with music
stevie wonder mixed
with barbara streisand
my daddy wears his dobb hats
on the weekends
my mom sometimes smiles
and is quieter than the walls
my fat nappy ponytails are separated
by one long part
a river flows through my head
i was born in this fountain
full of questions and confusion

balance

is not a loud sound
it is the realization
that humanity can be sung
if we find the instruments of truth

after being called pretty
for kevin powell

it's not that i haven't heard it before
well maybe not that
early in the morning

my teeth weren't brushed
my hair was wrapped in a red silk scarf
i bought in morocco
it was 8:30 am and i was on the floor of my
bathroom
bathing my 15 month old

i wasn't feeling pretty

not that pretty
is meaningful
or synonymous with smart

but it was the way he said it
like it was my name

the same way i'd been called

bitch

so many times
just days before

hello. pretty.

and i wonder if this makes me

needy
silly
inferior
vain

in need of therapy
self esteem building classes

when i have taught personal development

been the poster woman for
black woman defiance

my strength as thick as my used to be afro
my power manifested inside poems
my decade old company my activism

my b-girl stance.

still

pretty felt good

cause sometimes in the middle of
my exhaustion with niggas

who are stuck…

when you have dedicated your life to moving
toward change
while getting hated on because people

have to respect you
even if they don't like you

sometimes an independent revolutionary artist

woman

just needs a man to say

hello. pretty

thank her for simply existing
for participating in what prince called

this thing called life

cause being born and raised in
a place they call the most   dangerous city in the country

i realize it is a
short, precious thing

our people live in cities
that die a little more everyday

we have no respect for ourselves
our families

we fuck other people's wives, husbands
without thinking of their children

we live in a country that promotes the

ugly of war
the ugly of rape
the ugly of murder

we benefit from the blood of brown people
& use children as armor

why u think all the oil pipelines
run through the living rooms
of the chosen people

whose blood did u spill today?

maybe jesus was a muslim
he didn't pray to
god one day a week
after leaving the strip club at 4am

and faced the east?

the truth ain't always pretty
but damn

if it's all i got
this morning

then i will find a poem in it. a pretty bomb.

fuck it.

a mirror.

anything that'll wake us up while we
prepare to lie to our kids
about capitalism
during this holiday season

how many kids gonna die?
while we shop for christmas
gifts   even if we can't afford them

you can't convince me to cut down a tree
just to decorate it and watch it die
ruin my beautiful black son's imagination
waiting for a white guy to
bring him a wrapped up
lie

how many poor kids crying
cause they think they
must be bad

or all their letters to santa
ended up in tony medina's book?

and you wanna know what the hell
this has to do with a hello pretty
before 9 am
but you have to be a self evaluating
deconstructing your own existence
type thinker to understand

why that shit   just threw me off

brotha.

so next time you call me

call me

detroit read
jesse james
stressica
care moore
king's mama
somebody's wife
d-butterfly
just jess
sista

or maybe

just say

hello pretty

and i will write you a poem...

poem for amiri at 70

the death of my father at 69
reminds me
that every new year
is a kiss from god

or maybe it is simply a reminder
that catching bullets in our teeth
are not just for comic book super heroes
that literary giants also battle
against the monstrous alien heads of
connie and bill
and survive, unscathed.

your stories are that of a lion
on the frontline of an american schizophrenic jungle
prophet footing and warrior ink blood.

they cannot kill us all

with their black face and tragic twisted
imitations of life
we understand
amiri baraka has
out lived your double cross.

his books held political prisoner by
un-established unsophisticated establishments
we hold his words as armor
as a symbol of our fearlessness.

we ask his children, his wife, amina
for permission to claim him.

we smile his boyish grin
waiting for the low-ku
bomb to
        drop.

he teaches us there is jazz playing
every time the sun rises

adding a zero makes you faster
than the speed of sound

at 70
a jackal of words.
a blues man with his hat always in place
you
father of movement and possibility
baraka black and artistic
handing out pamphlets
full of rebellion and resistance

we know your lifework
is simply an answer to a question
why god?

why ancestors?

why malcolm?

why langston?

why sonia?

why amiri?

why in hell did you have to make

me

a poet?

and god replied,

"Leroi, somebody had to show them how to

do it!"

Happy Birthday amiri!

The day the devil died.
For ossie davis

It's amazing how a nudge in my arm
From this brilliant man sitting in this
Historic Harlem Church
Watching me from the pew
Noticing my nervous concern.
My wonder.
My outloud silent question.

How did I do?

And then him with beautiful intention
telling me:

You done good.

Helped changed my life.

And move more confidently past
All moments that feel this way.

Me, yellow sunflower ancestor
Detroit Red and Harlem living

Attempting Poet. Famous too soon.
Never famous enough.

Reading a slave narrative
Sharing a podium. A microphone.
The same space.

With a body of work.
A smile with ten thousand hellos.
Father of Theater
A voice with power
A voice I prayed for
when surrounded by white students
in a 4th grade classroom
And it was my turn to read aloud.

How I secretly conjured you and Malcolm
And searched for other women with a baritone
Sound.

Scratchy, loud, imperfect.

I wanted to make you proud.
And although I received praise and applause
That day in Harlem.
It was your elbow nudge

That helped me go home
And write my own narrative.

Bout my own fights with oppression
And the day the devil died.

for richard pryor

In my house
We didn't hide your records

They were displayed and regularly played
Usually on the record player on the basement bar
While my brothers played pool

I listened from the steps

It sounded like my daddy cussing
Only, *funnier.*

blues in black/mississippi with no phone
for kalamu ya salaam

where you think they got the idea
to wear dark glasses?

that sexy deep hiding place
cornea corrupted
quiet corner

girl interrupted by the noises
she keeps the voices close
in case of combat
or the wind blows too hard
her whole body shakes
whispers and owl screams
and tree-limbed whistles
climb to the top of her existence
a chance to steal a glimpse
of the beat down
the blue back reality of her mystery
and memory
compact covered,
microphone missled
jukebox grinning/long split
wearing/dandelion dressing/
automatic weapon/tear drowning
back water

mississippi river drankin'
the pain into a piss hole of oceans
and smiles and flour and sugar
in her bloodline
ain't she the anatomy of a blues poem?
don't she make the crowd call
ain't she the first and the last   laugh

sing/fly/shoot it up/forget
disappear inside the fever
dig your life into her silence
and be buried in discovery
as the music plays
the guitars practice their lives
her mouth is covered
she is the alley cat

she is being pushed into
her ballad is forced from behind
she cuts them with her eyes
her life-work
passion flower pulled from her own story
headliner for humanity
her blood
in your muddy river
exiled inside her own existence
you are free to   blow
        it
out

compose notes down her thighs
misinterpret/win
awards
for something that is a secret
only death can answer

who do you think taught those blues men
2 wear such dark glasses?
who told them this was a safe place?

oxford, mi february 28th @ 2:34 pm, mississippi blues conference.

For Radcliffe Bailey

Our memories are what make us human
Brown palms lined with tree branches
Slave ships dipped in black tar.

Nothing is more beautiful than the
Simplicity of black and white
Our pupils reflect the eye
Of a non-romantic Atlantic storm
Our short pants, our floods
That would kill and bring life
All at once.

Maybe it is the smell of upside down magnolias
Or the promise of fish that plays piano
Fueling our need to explain ourselves
In a language no one else
will understand.

Despite the torture of being lonely
We cover ourselves in this early morning blood
Sleeping inside beautiful Georgia cotton
We pray to find and love one more savannah sunrise
We eat the dirt/cooling digest colors
And smoke our afternoon cigarette
Blowing out something that will save us
Or keep us honest until tomorrow.

Remember the looking glass smiles back.

The blues is just a black hand-print
Against an uncertain sky
A compliment from a stranger
Who may want to kiss you.

We follow the black north star that led us
To this place that is cold, without imagination
The reason warm rum and spirit drinking
Helps us dance away the pain of
What they define as real.

Loss of familiar voices,
Will help you find your tongue
In a different place in your mouth

And new ways of explaining your life
Will begin

When silence haunts your nights
Your story will find you.

Every moment cannot be captured inside a frame
The collaged picture everyone sees is only what the
artist decides to show.

An inch above the knee
A centimeter below the heart
A piece of a smile
Hidden under a hat.

So please cover us in tar
And place our portraits beneath glass

Number my poems as people

Just don't leave the walls white
Bring wet brushes, anytime music
Words & feathers with knives

When I forget I am beautiful
I will dance
And when you forget you will paint
I will teach you
How to follow our red clay feet

Back to sacred ground.

warrior heart
for amina baraka

how many hearts do you have,
cherokee woman?
with your hand-made pottery
air-dryed miracles
smiling back at guests
on your living room mantle?

how can one be enough?
the way the world eats   hearts

i imagine you have at least 40.

1 in every finger
7 in your right brown arm
for brewing tea and cooking dinner
3 hide inside the palm of your
left hand, when fisted.
your left, long leg holds 5 more
your right is reserved for
newark street corner ghetto kung fu beat-downs.

2 sleep with one eye open
in the soles of your feet
so you can glide or float across floors
at public forums
even when you are tired
and don't feel like smiling.

six dance along your spine
to make the morning walk
there is one heart in each of your eyes
and 5 swimming in your womb.

that is why your hair is sometimes silver/blue
and your chest is never too heavy for others
to take over you.

you have back up
a chakra heart protection plan

just in case
        the vultures

                s
                    w
                        e
                            e
                                p
                                    through

84

I was going to ask you
a poem for sekou sundiata

I was asked by the National Black Arts Festival to host a conversation with one of my poetic fathers and musical inspirations, Sekou Sundiata. Unfortunately, Sekou died just days before his anticipated arrival to Atlanta in 2007. Instead, I would help put together a tribute.
this is the poem i wrote and shared that night.

I was hoping to ask you.

Where do you see the 51st Dream State?
I wonder if you are there now.
Are we free there?

Is it a physical place?
Is it a spiritual space?
Are there Afro-Caribbean drums playing?

Would you please leave us the road map?
These/us young poets are lost.
We are playing scrabble with no directions.
No dictionary/no history/no respect.

We want a double word slam score
With no skills with real letters.
That's why I'm so bored

with this game.

No, this gift.

Would you run for president with Barack
as your running mate?

That would be a beautiful poster.

Do they finally understand that we are

the dream

Sekou?

How do we thank you for your songs?

for thinking outside the box
for your grace.
Your Kwame Toure voice.
Your John Coltrane smooth rhythm.

You remind us all of our daddies
& long cadillacs and 125th street vendors
slick hats and go-tee gangsters.
Teach us how to do it, Sekou

With ease.
With tall Black man style.

Show them how to dress for the poem.
Conjure the ancestors
By simply waking up
and not just in the morning.
How to love
With a heart of glass.
With a stolen heart. A middle passage heart.
Kazi's heart.
A heart that beats to miles & writes
with the memories we aren't supposed to remember.

Teach us how to love with
A heart of brick
A house of pain
& shoes not easy to fill.

Sekou
So full of black stories
Biting away at this peculiar institution
with Griot tongue & emancipated language.

Atlanta needed you. More than any place in Europe
that would put your photo on the side of the bus or on
large billboards
& be able to deconstruct your work.
Or have heady discussions around your
life/work/your philanthropy/your performance.

We needed you. So we could better understand
who we are. We need more therapy for the
schizophrenia/the slavery/the self hate.

Cause we are all from the south at some point.
No DNA test necessary.
And you represent the continuum of our roots.
Our passion, our secrets, our survival, our bloodline.

I was going to tell you
That some of us
Knew you as the super hero Lang professor
With a double life.
A poet who translated our existence by night.

The brilliance of your sound.
The urgency of your message.
The importance of your existence.
The love in your heart.
The respect for your craft.

Will live on.
Inside the breath wind of Harlem children.
On the tide of every boat you have blessed.
Every student you have touched.
We will continue to live
Inside the blue one-ness of the dream
You always dreamt

for us.

I was going to ask you about all of this.
So now i have.

I can't wait to hear

your answers.

Pulling the Trigger
A poetic tribute to Ernie Paniccioli

In the beginning was the word
Poets with no mics
No radio and no hype
No magazines no rappers
with hooks
that sing.
The verse was the truth
And the meaning of
all things…

He was born   in between

Brooklyn and Cree
armed with lenses, camera
and shoulder strap.
He saw the history and importance of the boom bap.
Captured the spirit of this sound
Inside his lens cap.
What he shot would shock the world with it's relevance.
He understood the beauty of the crime.
He brought the evidence.
His foresight brought the news
Of future royalty
But the world stage didn't realize just
How this would come to be….

Birth of a nation
With no mammies.
Just griots
Who broke bread and beats.
The word unleashed
Blasted through neighborhood speakers
The church rocked shell toe sneakers.

Ernie understood
one day the world would need us.
The media would mistreat us
So he protected us
inside a different light.

A light with perspective and love
Brilliance and humility.

A light the devil recognizes as pure
Without pretension or zoom.

Hip Hop was born
In a world of dark rooms

And we loved the jazz be-bop in you.
The midnight marauder in you.
The rock and roll nigga in you.
The Afrika Bambaataa in you.
The flashy car, iced out confusion.
They continue to try to pump in you.
We can still recognize your heart.
Your Pete Rock, RZA, DJ Premiere beats..
We can feel you inside Quest Love's drum licks.

You helped me love my husband to the gangsta
dirty south music he creates.

You make my whole house shake.

They say you were born
in the Bronx
But you've been seen traveling through the
Children of Soweto.
Bouncing to your truth in
The streets of Brazil.
Dancing against the walls of Japan.

How many decades can one man
Capture inside the pupil
Of just one eye?

Can you carry that much weight
Inside the palm of your hands?

When you are a little girl
Listening to Run DMC and MC Lyte lacing up
Your thick laces.
You think you can
Out-run the planet.
You know that this is the soundtrack
you walk to
Breathe to
learn to love to.

And like all little girls in love one day
You will figure out that even when it sounds pretty
Doesn't mean it won't hurt you.
Catch you off guard
Like nodding your head to a song that portrays
You as simple, a hoe, a sack chaser, an object.
So you deconstruct and play the track back
You find a way, despite your pain
To find the love in it.

Can you picture that?

It was the only thing that made sense when you
Dreamed of rocking the mic
While memorizing all the words to Fight The Power.
Why you gave up beef after listening to Kris Parker.
It's the reason why your Maurice Malone baggy jeans
used to hang low to hide your shape
so you could get respect
when your voice touched the mic.
You understood violence
was apart of the world.
So you armed yourself inside the music
Found solace.
Wrote your own stories, rocked your own bells
And fly Kangols.
Stayed protected on the mic when Rakim killed 21 emcees, when
Crazy
Legs spun in circles on the floor,
Armed with Keisha's complex graffiti, and Jam Masters Jay scratches.
You could outlive your circumstance.
You can define yourself outside the label of whore/poor/urban.
Invisible and silenced in your country.
You thought your track suit had wings
And this mystical thing
That pushed you close to the edge
Helped you escape the gunshots of your streets
With your headphones tight on your ears.
You could hear liberation
ancestors speak back.
A gritty speaking of tongues, a scientific language
Only you and your people understood.

You never pictured someone taking your picture
While you were just trying to live.

Contorting your body into a b-girl stance
To help you get down the street
Or build your self-esteem.

Ernie proves that we were/are here.
That we smiled and mean mugged.
That we grew, switched rhyme styles.
And some of us wear suits.
Others prefer black face.
While the field emcees search for independence.
Three decades later
We're fighting against the colonization
Of an art form we created and lost
To barbie girl groups and big screen idiot boxes.
We need more MC-EO's
To keep these thieves out our temple's pockets.

I wrote this for Ernie.
Beautiful mentor and friend
To our generation.
Because Legends aren't ever honored
or paid what they are worth
While they are still alive
And you can still get them
on the phone.
The lie of fame and industry gossip
Is far more interesting then paying attention
To someone who can actually
change your life or teach you
something.

We are all hypocrites.
The world's beautiful antagonists.
Hood historians, battle rhyme magicians,
Capitalistic, misogynists, debate champions,
Comedians, actors, poets, politicians,
activists and hustlers.
We bring balance.
We are corn-rolled parents
Parting our babies heads down the middle
With green grease and black combs.
Telling them stories about the "real" Hip Hop.
Singing "It's like that..and that's the way it is."
We are young and already old school.
Afro puff blowing/patent leather Adidas sportin/ trendsetting/funky

sweat hanging off a biggie t-shirt.
late night concert arriving/laughing aloud/crying when no one's
looking/stage loving/
revolutionary
creators
of the blue light in the basement party.

Children of the "Genesis"
Labeled Hip Hop by the labeling committee.
Surviving so many storms.
Babies of the civil rights movement
Who stretched far beyond the norm.

Thank you Ernie for
More proof of life.
For being our reflection in a world
Surrounded by false mirrors.
You are the grandmaster with your flash.
The magnificent hills of sugar
Memorialized inside the mountain of your film.

Thank you for taking our 35 millimeter picture
When no one else was looking.
We remember when radio didn't play us
And our street corner freestyles
Never went past our block, or that moment
You documented our time
standing still   shots.

And I pray you never quit, Ernie Paniccioli
Even when we betray our own portraits.
Our incredible history.
Turn our backs on our roots.
Forget the fire.

People are dying to be heard
To be seen
all over the world.
And I gotta find a poem
To fit inside one of your pictures.
One that matters more than this moment.
Somewhere under my skin
Below my neck,
Inside my throat
Deep in the pit of my stomach.

I don't know what the others will do
When the earth cracks in two
Or the sun finally gets too close.
When the oceans, tornadoes, volcanoes,
Hurricanes and rainforests
Come for revenge.
As we sip our morning paper
And read our premium coffee.

When our addiction to nothing
Finally goes away, but

I know you will be there

Shooting our pain.
Exposing our possibilities.
Loving our glory.
Explaining our expressions.
Our peace signs.
Our war chants.
Our subtleties.
In black and white
Our complexities
In full color.

Maybe it was your mothers love that saved you
Or the library that empowered you.
Or living on the streets of New York City that
Propelled you
To keep shooting us
From a spiritual perspective.
To honestly love
what you were
shooting
right before you decided
to pull the trigger.
I shot ya.

for tupac shakur

in a time of war
they kill the poets first
for knowing their enemy
and calling them by their first names
crooked cops and c.i.a.
you reminded us
murder is the american way.

attempting to live is an act of violence
when you are young black and gifted
touched by angels and silenced.
nation building with words
rapid fire tongue as your weapon
son of a warrior who fought through oppression.

america's nightmare
they'll steal your hype, but never your heart
so smart, we heard you in detroit
telling us you'd answer if we called.
we felt you in new york when brenda had a baby
we loved you in high rise projects
and low rider cars in cali
we listened on college campuses and down south weed spots
because we were trapped too
and you said and did things many of us
were scared to
being born black in this country
makes you an automatic rebel
you understood the power of keeping your head up
in the face of the devil
your last words heard round the world
even a genius asks questions
how many poems should we write
to undo the lessons?
how many beautiful songs before we reap all the blessings?
brick walls birth brick people
some chose corners when they couldn't find preachers
should i be scared to tell my truth
if my truth can one day kill me?
even the politicians are trickin
and my own people can't really feel me.
you told us
holla if ya hear me

in the absence of love, we call for god
you understood being a black male
makes living hard
if we "die tonight" we're resurrected by your songs
apostles, martyrs, prophets, pimps, poets and all y'all.

my girls were good girls
with no protection from this world
at close range we drove by blood
left on black picket porches
we poured out a little liquor
they're scared we're carrying your torches
we scream for mercy and bang your tracks
we light candles, and try to rewind time back
we know the government is the thug
and we all know who you are
so we're spiritually strapped
cause the future ain't far
is there a heaven for poets?
when do lyrics turn into prayers?
we still playing your music
searching for you between the lines there.

what they hate about you
they hate more about themselves.
they see the best of prophets
and keep em contracted and shelved.
they can see the riches in death
but we know the wealth of your life
wonder how you walked
with your back full of knives.
it ain't easy when you got words of wisdom
with the pain of love & bullets dropped in ink
three strike rules makes it real hard to think.
a revolutionary souljah's story
never too many too tell
you were born by the river
your wishes too big for this well.
so many tears
so many inspired by
your black songs
your manhood
your smile like malcolm
in the face of death.
tupac amaru shakur

cradle to the grave
tradin war stories
life goes on
no more pain
i ain't mad at cha
tha lunatic
part time mutha
something wicked
2 of amerikaz most wanted
temptations
young niggaz
lord knows
heavy is the game
ghetto star
how do you want it
old school
outlaw
i wonder if heaven got a ghetto
letter to the president
dear mama
black cotton
heartz of men
strugglin'
hail mary
who do you believe in?
against all odds
redemption
black jesuz
breathin'
only god can judge me
where do we go from here?
when i get free
everything they owe
2pacalypse now
guess who's back
tupac, in this time of war
we will never forget.

"i don't know how to teach inspiration. but, somehow, sometimes, there is that break-thru moment when you make a mistake and actually inspire"

—jcm

recipe for survival
for sonia sanchez at 71

the year of my birth
you wear
smooth as silk and feathers
water voice and theater hands
easy
on the road.
paris, detroit, philly, dallas
on sunday you will sleep
watch a comedy to boost
your immune system.

i call you to thank you for the organic
fruit, almonds, strawberries and apples
that taste like apples.

teach me to survive
being a poet
at 33.

give me the strength
to schedule in our breathing
on fridays
so we can teach on saturday.
sign books for three hours
and smile.
remember why we write
take time to get better.
live enough hours
to create new stories.

1 part water 2 tablespoons of aloe vera juice
mornings mixed with apple cider vinegar.

always honey
always sweet

to see you so full of moonlight
in my hometown.

talking about our generation and yours
these motor city streets blending
with the sound of your voice.

you a poet/woman with swagger
integrity and love
& you give me no reason not to continue
to search for our humanity

inside hand-me down poems
or recipes for survival

when you are born in this skin
in this place.

they call america.

what do we have
left to pass down
more
important   *than love?*

The Words Don't Fit in My Mouth
Remix Intro

i'm the flame cracklin in a sunday newspaper
stick bon fire on detroit's west side
blues songs strum along pink and yellow candy necklaces
held together by white string
turning into blue collar for hire.

i am a convertible green cadillac
and my hair don't blow straight
belle isle park and paten leather adidas
shine my seven and a half foot fetish for black top
i'm 24…well..35….
trying to stop writing these poems about home.

i'm six two on the weekends
and blacker than the bluest eye
i'm a woodward avenue hoe before gentrification
looking for a new ride
to the old tiger stadium

i'm a pimped out 67 impala with metallic blue
and silver lion trim

i'm a church fan in love
with all my teams even

when they lose.

i'm the pride of the black south moving north to find work
i'm from an assembly line of colored girls
writing chrome and steel poems about home.

Smoke
(for my dear friend, who taught me how to be revolutionary)
remembering u. yale guy miller *(njoma)*

in honor of returning home
after 12 years in the desert.

when i smoked a clove for the first time
it was for the taste it left behind on my lips.

if i was gonna smoke   anything
it had to be sexy
it had to serve a purpose.

i have the same approach to writing poetry
and loving the men i have loved.

just leave me something good on my mouth
a nice word behind my ear.
something i can bite down on and remember

years later.

i've decided.

when i grow up.

i'm going to drink wine.
i'm going have a mysterious wine cellar.
i'm going to know the origin of the grape.
i'm going to grow my own vines
and tell stories to my children through
one long_____drunk line.

i'm going to learn to use a corkscrew
i'm going to be a person who takes a
small sip and smells the glass

but today i'm more of a tequila shot girl
a graduate from the eighties
hennessey and vodka.

i really just want something sweet.
easy to digest. slow. purposeful.

something that tastes so good
just the thought of it makes me high

when i become my full warrior self.

i will be a woman with an unbreakable spirit

101

dream catchers for arms alligator boots
poems without curses
poems never written
in this slave language.

i won't be a pretty girl
who needs to be reminded
she's pretty

but we do. don't we   ???

all detroit girls are good stock.
we hit the potholes and keep riding

we born driving.

i can feel the sadness of my city
waiting for someone to claim it
in a box marked lost and found.
i can drink down this room
and piss out the motown sound.

i can eat engines and command an eagle.
i am black and detroit and regal.
i am flashy with long cars and
piped out trucks.

my walks demands a "what up."

i am a "doe"
in a forest of cows.

i am an 88 benz with heated seats.
i am a ford pickup truck
that drives like an escort with
some extra shit in the back.

never keep the tags on
cause i don't do take backs.

when i am born again
i will know who really has my back.

this city makes me want all our daddies back.

tom moore
harry taylor
george woods
larry ray robinson
ashe'

little tom, lisa, pat
ang lex
charlotte
tureka

we all daddy's girls with no daddies

we a city made for caddies
killing people's daddies.

my coming home is finally not
for a funeral.

i am returning to a place of war.
i am returning to a place of love.

a wasteland with new lofts downtown.
a holy place with schools and no books.
abandoned neighborhoods & beauty
beyond belief.

we used to cut the grass in the ghetto.

it's deep to be the only one at the after
hours bar

who's not drinking?

smoking

crack
heroin

popping
ex pills

mufflers
chimneys
exhaust pipes

fire station number one
can you save us from this chemical waste
when the lie of gentrification
goes up in smoke?

the new billboard off the lodge expressway:

detroit rock city
rock and roll niggas
jesus was a muslim

the heart of our city is on fire.

when i heard yale was murdered
charlotte heard it on wjlb

yale murdered   here?

in this city that he loved.
that he nurtured.
that he represented all over the world?
that he saved lives in.

something inside me
caught on fire
and i can't help the
power of what follows…

what gives birth
what poems i write
what poison i drink to help
destroy all this devil night heat

what makes the wind blow
that hard when we are

closer to the river.

i trust in karma
i know the devil   personally.

she wears fake prada.

when i came home

(this time)

it was for the taste
detroit left behind

on my lips.

there are repercussions
for loving this way

for so many years..

& i am no longer afraid

of what comes up
with
the smoke.

going home

for jazz legend shelia jordan. after breakfast
in toulouse, october 25, 2002

3 days before 31
in the south of france
my return home is so unsure. so scattered
i sink into my velvet jogging suit
burnt orange like my hair.
tears come with morning
smiles are easy. sometimes forced.
i only eat pomme frites
and drink chocolat au chaud
what else is there? i wonder.
maybe life is the road. traveling and spinning
sneaking into first class. train rides through europe
and postcards home to my mum.

when will she leave detroit?
a photographer snaps my picture
as i write this poem.
silent. alone.
surrounded by
echoes of white walls
i need to listen to more jazz, i think.
james from fertile ground told me he would
find the music to convert me.
i examine the miles davis paintings on the wall
he is blue and splashed against the large canvas
like most black men
i'm learning about perspective
and circumstance and the smallness of the world.
i sat to the right of this woman in black
who spoke of jazz and harlem in one sentence.
i asked if she was a new yorker
sensing her difference from the chelsea area she
lived for years.
i even spoke of my first, as if it was home.
but we both escaped another city.

the french black city of detroit
woodward and euclid
tireman and ward.
we exchanged streets and stories
while drinking tea and pretending to eat.

chasing mingus was a good reason to go
or maybe it was simply the racism
the threats against our lives
the inability to breathe in car exhaust.
maybe it was my daddy dying at 69 in 1994
just a few days after the new year
that sucked the beauty and music out of our homes.

when we spoke, it was clear.
in order to live, at some point we had to move
away from the confusion of segregation.
we needed to crawl inside an upright bass
our fingers camouflaged inside the strings.
where do little girls full of blues
go when they're city won't allow them to
sang, or write poems in their own language.

escaping detroit is never easy.
you dream of rosa and west grand blvd.
concrete streets and our canadian border.
hudson's and magic and Motown.
you are the pimp walk of curved streets
and chrome and steel.
who will drive your get-a-way car?
the racist cops the riots the gunshots
the enormous potholes
will ruin your tires.

we tell you about the continuum
and you speak of the black poets
the guitar sounds of garrison.
i was born inside dudley and margaret
haki leroi and sonia.
you are happy to know some of us are still
writing ourselves into existence

i look so tired to be young.
you look so young at 74

following jazz to the beat down
streets of nyc.
i think i was running
a bag of poems and all my belongings
in my purple ford pickup.
some choose to escape

when everyone is sleeping.
we left in broad daylight
threw a party at the underground railroad.
tickets were free
and years later
we're still trying to be.

realizing detroit never leaves your spirit
as we dance along the world
we've carved out of acoustic faith and
kinetic connection to the souls of black folks.
somehow we meet ourselves along the way
in other forms, inside a song, different languages.
perhaps even today
in the south of france
we are reminded of why we left
and why for the rest of our lives
we will always return
(effortlessly)

to the gritty birthplace of our art
that couldn't contain or control
the capacity
of our hearts.

keisha's complex graffiti
for b-gyrls

i ride trains.
complex graffiti.
8:30 up early
the whole day feels me
deals me devils.
i'm packed with aerosol angels.
my speech is tangled.
walk with switches.
conductor blows me kisses
camouflaged inside the ditches.
we ride dirty.
jesus hair curly.
hungry nigga painting pictures
with his trigga.
i smoke a black ciga.
my mind fucks with things
my body can't give you.
outlive you
cause death brush bigger.
no basements with tigger.
real underground hurt u.
even rats will desert you.
no time to alert you
we blastin' before street lights and curfews.
nobody move.
we selling stories for food.
don't fuck with me.
i'm in a good mood.

i rhyme in color.
take over liquor store walls.
hear the bird calls.
hold up
the popo's checkin' the halls.
we duckin' them all
setting it off.
don't hestitate when u cough.
your last word
may be the breath that you lost.
picture me deep in the moss.
see your canvas and i'm checkin' you off
a purple haze/my girls blaze

cause we set in our ways.
honor roll fades
but to the streets we get grades.
sign our own name
never descendants of slaves.
the blacker hearts brave
before the cave.
here's the diamonds i saved.
gimme back all the black pussy you crave.
you can't have no more dave.
paint a picture of josephine days.
back door till you get us on stage.
shake the can and the picture don't change.
we just hide in the fame.

the government won't recognize the heroes we claim.
give malcolm his day
for all the bullets they sprayed.
so many die the same way
in the middle of day/lights/camera.

can u picture me saved?
speaking in tongues   sunday morning
mama may have, but goddess bless the girl
that knows this ain't home.
read between the space in the comb.
our legacies corn rolled.
hard to imagine us growing old.
keep bombing till the truth be told.

you know my name is keisha
and the things i draw come true
they take me take me take me…

detroit, this morning.
canorous was the dictionary word of the day.

detroit, this morning

the canorous beat of his heart forced me to hear motown songs
everytime i took a step, or inhaled this bitter cold
attempting to kill me and save me all at once.
this is the melody
of my life.

i blow frost from my mouth
and the song is a circle, a heart, my son's name
against the window
against the air
these words can cut
transfrom this place
into what i need it to be.

this is the power of sound
& the beauty of silence.

60 mile an hour winds
cannot win against the canorous
whistle of my teapot.

i will not be moved.

breathing in
& pushing out

the city

where i was born.

Even the light skinned girls
are sick of the light skinned girls
(for dream hampton)

In south Africa. The radio disc jockey says:

You can get killed for speaking that way in this country.
The government doesn't mess with you for reading poems
Like that or speaking that way in America?

They kill us. They ruin our credit. As soon as we get to
College. They make it harder to live in invisible ways.

It is a slow death.

The colored girl cries cuz
I'm not telling her story

Right.

I am colored here. It is difficult to explain
Myself/ourselves. Isn't it? Black so black and
Yellow and Native and
Twisted. And confused.

I was raised in Tom Moore's house.
I was raised in Master Moore's house.
My daddy was black native Motown southern
Cadillac African loud on purpose big smile.
Dimples called the white boys at the Canadian
Borders
Niggers.

My daddy with rifle on porch during the riots
Took my Canadian raised quiet mother down
south in the 60's
In his convertible Cadillac.

My aunts told her to stay in the house.
She didn't understand this was not a safe
Place. For love. Loud like my daddy's.

This is the education they didn't teach my young mother
On the Canadian news.

I've never been down with those crumpled bags of
Paper/ tests of blackness.
The red blood and high cheeks of
My people
Don't subscribe to this psycho drama
jim crow south africa mississippi

divide and

divide and

conquer the red clay boom bap jazz.
deconstruct the hip hop nigga you heard me.
destroy the slave whip before the slave ship.
yoga your way out

of this chaos across oceans this ugly that
connects us. High yellow girl in South Africa
my daddy is from Alabama.
1920's cotton
in harlem we are all just Puerto Ricans
it don't matter. Say Hola! Got dammit

you know me. Little girl. I am your sister
this shit don't even exist. They made it
exist in a nightmare to steal your gold.
The poverty is what they left inside those
Books.

You are golden. With broken eyes. Circling me
An ambush of pupils trying to get me to get you.

But I am you.

You talk like a white girl.

You.

Black at the white school.

You.

Love your white family.

You

Don't know nothing else.

You don't have to choose a side.
You a whole woman.
You a whole person
You ain't multi ethnic diversity
Class poster child.

You are a whole heart. An entire lung
You breathe in humanity. You just a baby
Being born. You just an ancestor covered
By skin.

My ancestor was a dark chocolate West African woman.
She said she just wanted to see what it felt like. Said it
Was okay, but something was missing.
So she scarred my face to
give me edge.

I see your scars 2
child holding your fathers hands.
I'm sorry I am not the mirror you asked for.

I am also my father's child.
I am who I say I am.
Obama is a Black man.
He is
Who he says he is.

This is not a privilege
This is political choice.

Even the light skinned girls
are sick of

The light
skinned girls…

The Call To Prayer is A Hip Hop Beat

I was walking inside a mall in Dearborn, which borders Detroit. when i was young my mother and her best friend, both white women with black husbands and children, both boycotted dearborn. they didn't want "detroiters" in their pools, parks and city in general. dearborn is where i learned some pieces of arabic, and which red berries were safe to eat. when my hair was wet in the pool, they didn't quite know what to think..till it was dried up into a kinky afro. then it was clear. me and sister were from the other d.

so. years later, i'm in the mall, and this young girl is in the elevator with me speaking fluent arabic and checking out a necklace around my neck. she said she'd never seen anything like "that" before.

i grew up across the street from islam.
two worlds. one palm.
little girl with covered hair.
isis stare. skin fair.
watch the hijab head nob.

when i found islam
the call to prayer was sleeping
inside a hip hop beat.
covering up and dressing modest
meant some baggy jeans and a maurice malone
fear allah or genes like jesus logo.

islam wasn't just brown people from the middle east.
they weren't just the arab men who owned liquor stores in our neighborhoods
the men who flirted with black girls
and we never saw their wives.

islam was idris black and smooth.
ishmael yellow and cool.
it was fly sistas who could rhyme
wrap their hair in raw silk
and stop you with their walk.
it was azzah who designed clothes from
potatoes sacks.

it was hasaan. the dancer,
full time allah promoter.
a walking billboard

a salesman for detroit.
for change.

sometimes we were muslim hoodlums.
we were detroiters.
we drove cars and brought our prayer mats
to school in our backpacks.

how many christians you know pray five times
a day with 18
credit hours??

islam was the hip hop shop open mic
with dj sabotage or dj head spinning.

islam was proof
in a freestyle battle against busta rhymes
when he was still with leaders of the new school.

that was st. andrews hall.

so years later when a young girl from
lebanon was riding in an elevator with me
and my son and her mother

at fairlane town center in dearborn.

openly talking about the large symbol of
allah bling i was sporting round my neck

i had to involve myself in the conversation.
i was clearly not the hip hopper from 93.
i was grown with a baby stroller
tight jeans and uncovered braided hair.

i asked her if she was talking about my necklace.
and she was taken off guard, but excited that i'd
said something.

she said "yes," then asked if i was muslim.

this is the time when you always say yes jess.

the other time is when the jehovah witnesses are
at the door.

she asked if i was from africa. morroco maybe?

said she had never seen anything like that before.

anything like what?

you never saw a black girl with the light of
islam around her head?

you've never seen her breakdance pose into
her prayer position.

you never threw a snowball across to the
other side of tireman sis?

don't you know allah doesn't belong to you alone?
to dearborn. to the middle east. to any race or
culture or gender or hairstyle or fundamentalist group for that matter?

and that's when i remembered how i found
islam inside hip hop.
how i found stokely and farrakhan and sonia
and malcolm and assata and all the voices
of resistance.

and i wondered if this little girl would've seen
all of this if she would've just had the nerve
to simply cross

the street.

Will they call it a Jazz Funeral?

Will they call it a Jazz Funeral?
Will they drum at Congo Square?
Will the Mississippi River be
drunk with guilt?

Will the president seek revenge
On Mother Nature?
Smoke her out?
Shoot her children?
Watch them beg for help?
Fly around them in helicopters?
Leave them to drown.

Is this Apartheid?
Huh?
Is this Democracy?
How?

Maybe he will just move slow
Remember, this is the "big easy."
He'd show up five days too late
Wearing a Mardi Gras mask
With no spirit.
Plastic & paint & lies pouring from
His mouth.
A head to hang on the door, for out of town guests
A mule, a slave-traders ancestor
An oil refinery as his toilet water
His shit stinks.
His government has lost it's mind.
It's people.
.
The American Red Cross
Is parked in another state
Waiting for the people of New Orleans
To find their way to them.

We need the underground railroad.
We need a trolley car to freedom.

European affluent white tourists begin to
loot the French Quarter Walgreens
On the corner of Royal and Iberville

After watching the milk and cheese spoil
In 90 degree heat for days.

This will not make the news.
Looting is a capitalistic curse word.

Jim Crow is in effect in 2005.
Mississippi River is the new racial divide.
If you're poor and black
You'll never make it to the other side.
Martial Law for some, if you're rich you'll be fine.
I watch some families reunite via private jets.
There are hundreds of babies with no parents yet?

The greatest superpower in the world
Dropping food on their citizens
Into a river of toxic waste!
Working people referred to as refugees
America, a national disgrace.

25,000 body bags
Waiting to be filled.

Is this the Holocaust?
Is this Halliburton?
Is this a wake up call or a nightmare panic?!
How many flowers dying in the attic?

Will they call it a Jazz funeral?
Will they drum at Congo Square?

If they were your children
How long would it take for you to get there?

How many soldiers still fighting in Iraq?
While America runs out of gas and water
They turn their backs on the lives
Of beautiful, oh so black southern daughters.

Will they call it a jazz funeral?
Will they drum at Congo Square

I'm looking for America
I think I saw her...over there...

Drowning...

The Second Middle Passage

For the people of New Orleans.

this is not the first middle passage
of our people.
just another blessing a sacrifice
a question from god
that tests our integrity.
our strength is only in how
we answer back.

it defines our humanity.

from the ivory coast to the gulf coast
to the west coast.

black folks have always had a special
relationship with water

to baptize our spirits
to bathe our babies
to heal our wounds
to carry us to the promise land.

water has carried us to freedom
when no one was watching

water was our compass back to ourselves
when we were stolen.

water was our reminder that there was
something greater on the other side.

water became something we ran from only as
americans.

so, i understand when the weather man
said a hurricane by any name was coming

some of us cooked gumbo.
some of us sat on our rocking chairs
and passed down a new story.
some of us played the numbers
and some of us told our children

a storm is coming.

at 9:38 am when the london canal broke
our hearts became flooded by water.
fathers searched for higher ground.
mothers wrapped themselves around their
babies.

many were separated.

some of our elderly were home alone.
many still lost.

what's the cost to rebuild a superdome
but not the families of the sick and displaced
who died there?

again,
this is not a new history for our people.
our angels are always among us
waiting for our safe return to the shore.
the lower ninth ward remains
a deserted waste land ignored
by promises to rebuild.
but some of us ain't leaving
some of us will turn to brick and
be the foundation for new homes.

new orleans teaches us how to live
to pay homage to the music of the sun every morning
our homes are in our own hands
the blues print swimming in the lines of our palms.

how many years does it take to
recognize the chosen people?
to walk on this wetland soil
and feel the resilience carrying us
with every step with every raindrop.

new orleans is the world's imagination
a mardi gras mask never removed
we need the underground railroad to tennessee st.
we need a trolley car to freedom.

the new normal has to include the native

people, the poor, the artists, the local
front porch historians
who make this city great.

beneath the piles of debris and wood panels of
used to be homes
lies our people's legacy.

billions of dollars in federal aid
and seventeen thousand still living in trailers.

we need public schools with clean running water
we need hospitals and bridges
jobs and reconstruction.

of course we felt katrina coming
our legs were tired from running from
400 centuries of storms.
we listened to the wind & prayed
for ancestors to make it pass us by.

we knew the levees were weak
we didn't think they would break.

still, we don't have to be home owners
to know this is our land.

we don't have to have insurance
to understand our vast culture our people
our coast

is one of this country's
greatest natural resources.

our blood and freedom and secret
recipes for survival
our rituals our religion
our mississippi god damn black.

we african mermaid land walkers
why would we leave our homes
our crawfish stories our jazz music
so rich northerners can buy our
neighborhoods after ours are washed away?

we may not always know how to swim
but we are not afraid of water
unless we're just leaving the hair salon.

i heard someone called us
refugee

today tourists pay to ride along
graveyards beneath wood and steel.
they take pictures with indifference.
our dna numbered and calculated
by the letter x.
on the side of homes.
the pride of a neighborhood swept
beneath the rug of this governments guilt.

where is the money?

in the pockets of politicians
stuck to the red tape of programs
offering 700 dollars to rebuild your entire life.

from florida avenue to bourbon street

we are still here.
a musical composition of african and french
& down south dirty.
our breath inside the saxophone
our curves camouflaged inside the bass
a trumpet filled with water & life.

we are survivors.
if we are on the corner we are fish
swimming upstream not lost.
we a spicy jambalaya you can taste before you eat.

the 17th street canal water
should lead us back home.

this iconic city will not be buried in
under water graveyards..
we will not let them forget.
we will rise above the tide.
nearly two thousand souls
deserve our dedication.

their suffering will not be in vain.

as our unquestionable president explains this is not
his home and he only visits a few times out the year
like the rest of us..
to eat some of the nation's best food

so he can see the progress.

i must digress

when it is your family drowning
and struggling to rebuild their lives
you no longer have the right or
luxury of being tourist

especially when you name yourself leader.

we must be nation builders
water bearing warriors
with our babies on our backs
and our shovels in our hands.

invisible women

*i read this at the united nations world aids day event.
i remember being nervous because I spoke after kofi anan. As I
read the poem, I wondered if he was listening.*

this is a poem for invisible women

those beautiful
creatures created in your likeness

those magic bag story tellers

those nation builders.

those who grow vegetable gardens in the desert. those twilight women

who

hide in trees and wait. who hunt. who gather. those candle lighters.

mystic

wolves. native griots. southern tongue. wide-hipped. african born.

alabama

removed. geographically displaced. hair always in place. perfect.

distraught. poverty stricken. invisible warrior women. camouflaged
limbs in the strings of a harp. invisible.

those grandmothers, those sisters, those mothers, those aunties, those

caregivers, those sun reflectors, those earth drivers, those born

today, yesterday, tomorrow, this second.

those god. the ones who teach us to love the unloved. to remember
we

are a royal people. she is in trouble. god. goddess. prophets. hail mary.
queen sheba. nzinga. oya. tara. hetsepshut. she. she. kali durga black
madonna great mother. fatima. is dying.

she.god.

is dying.

in silence. by the thousands. at knifepoint. without protection. in

alleys. in her own home. in bathrooms. in school. by teachers. by men in uniform. by her own father. her uncle. her boyfriend. her first love. her last love.

her first kiss is with bloodshed. she is a soldier for this. she was just trying to find the love in it, like all girls do. searching for god in a man, instead of her throat or heart.. she wanted to feel like a woman. whole. like her mother. who lives in fear. a fear she will soon know as the way it simply is here. when you are invisible.

this is her body. she wanted to scream at 12. she is not ugly, she repeated in the mirror at 14. she cannot stand up at 17. she is a water sign with no water. their our thieves in her temple. there is no fortress to protect her from herself. she is at the mercy of others. being born girl is a sin, they say. bury it. hide it. burn it with acid. give it no resources. this is a slow death.

make her throw it up after dinner or hide the bruises behind dark glasses at work. she will make it the pain she deserves. she will blend guilt with her food and feed it to her daughters. she will tell them to smile in the dark and never dream out loud.

this is your inheritance. keep it under your tongue. quietly. kenya. every 30 minutes. say a prayer. which?

place this locket under your pillow. don't talk about the rape. huh?

wrap it around your neck like umbilical cord.

where?

turn blue.

why?

most of you are black anyway.

why do they want to kill off the women. eve?

first?

who will water the ocean?

who will balance the universe?

who will serve the tea? cook the meal? feed their sons?

whose backs then?

tell her it is a gift, not property. tell her she owns it and it is not

for

sale. tell her—her color is sacred. tell her that her strength can

stop

wars. tell her this is not her war alone. that her reflection is there,

she

just can't see it yet.

she is a phoenix. a panther. a thunderbolt of passion paralyzed by her

circumstance. she lives and will die the statistic you study.

she. like an animal is being called an endangered species.

they are children god. nearly two million in sub-saharan africa.

given butterfly wings and hiv during delivery. breastfeeding has become
lethal.

we are failing our girls. our daughters. left out of the trinity of our
prayers. we bomb the earth and arrogantly forget this is our womb.
our birthplace is being mutilated with our legs and arms held down.
injected with dirty needles. carved up with used knives. without
armor or western medicine. we spoiled, turn our backs in our own
beginning.

america, how can we turn our back on mother africa.
you have mined her diamonds, worn her gold, drilled her oil, enjoyed
her oceans. enslaved her people, her history. how can we not save africa's
greatest natural resource.
african women.

there is a fire on the river. we have banned her heat from existence.

her laughter. her books. her right to freedom over her own body. her longing for an education is considered contraband.
we owe it to invisible women everywhere to fight harder. to all african

women. to the women of asia, south america, india, china, soweto, zambia, zimbabwe, botswana, kenya, peru, Jamaica, afghanistan and the nearly 80% of african american women living with aids in the u.s.

to ensure the safety of girls.

the plight of women. determines the survival of humanity.

we have to find them. through the door of no return. inside the wind.

inside

our churches, our mosques, our synagogues, our temples, our homes, our backyards, our doorsteps, behind curtains, dark glasses, next to flowers, inside the dirt, digging through garbage, inside a smile, behind a tear drop, inside the rainfall, between the hurricanes, inside volcanoes, in the heart of storms, the ricochet of gunshots, the abortion clinics, the after-hours, the pool halls, the lunchrooms, the place between love and hate, under our noses, inside our books, our workshops, our classrooms, our elitism, our religions, our politics, our individualism, our capitalism, our revolutionary songs.

we have to give them power. the courage they gave freely. to say no. to choose. to fight against their own social norms. we must fight against gag orders aiding in our need for information, protection and prevention.

remind them when goddess worship was scripture. push outside the boundaries of neighborhood, of country, of gender, of sexual orientation, of race, of generation, of culture, of reflection.
we have to tell them we can hear the earth cry for help on this night. the 10,000 that died this morning. we know you by name. yes. you. warrior. survivor. those born today. not yesterday. not tomorrow. not invisible. at this second.
you are here. in this room. magic invisible women.

i see them everywhere. do you?

color of soul poem

june 29, 2003

souls with the gift of second sight.
souls split in twos
somewhere between ethiopian sunrise & egyptian mathematics
these souls spoke in tongues-red
as chinese ribbon
spicy souls in the form of latin dance
or boogie down bronx drums.
through the door of no return
ivory coast \ souls \ stolen
swimming souls, with no fins.
drowning souls with no water.
american souls with no soul at all.

the soul of a black artist, sad and confused.
defiant and renegade funk soul.
dancing and singing and writing about our blackness
when blackness is not abstract or is it?
the color of funk and sweat and southern rain.

when the black soul you wish to touch has
evaporated into unrecognizable colors
dancing in off beat rhythms without a soul or memory
or pictures or roots past their inner city blues.
the bought, lost and sold souls of clarence
the blue eyed black girl with silicone breasts
the bone of spine, the twist of lies
a black man forgetting to walk upright.
the schizophrenic american soul with quadroon dualities and
colonized languages with no state flower or extinct animal to claim.

muddy river soul.
alabama red clay souls. murdered souls. prison industrial complex
souls. souls that have walked across brown rivers and hidden inside
century old gullah trees.

the color of a soul line that starts wars and births children.
divides cultures and neighborhoods and money.
the frontline souls of blood and wars.
the new born soul of a black child born free.
the souls speaking morse code inside tap shoes griots.
the soul of an emcee. the freedom fighting soul. the soul of a poet.

zora neale's search for soul-thropology.
the black and blue eyed pea soul, boiled rice, collards, the souless

pig, the scraps, yams, grits, drippings, dressings, that saved us before tofu, and soy burgers and fake cheese. maybe the 80's pot roast with potatoes, the midwest mashed potatoes and green beans, the french fries and taco bells and mickey d's and kfcs that market us a deep fried death. maybe our souls are not baked in ovens after all.

the dictionary definition of soul. #11 please see soul music. american music is soul music, playing with blind ray eyes and james brown capes, and blue light in the basement parties, the thrust of momma's switch, the boom box sound of motown soul, of smokey nights and marvin and diana singing out her brewsters project window, the p funk soul of the mothership, the charlie parker—pete rock-reminiscing soul sample, the slow jam, aretha franklin anything, sparkle, the first kiss, our heart break, our singing in the shower concerts, our doo-wop, stevie's harmonica, michael's thriller jacket, and my daddy's convertible green cadillac, the teena marie, where'd she come from soul!

soul is the color of air and skylines and deep forests and twilight children and drunken laughter and haunted daylights and hallucinating black cats and voodoo rituals and catholic school communions, baptist baptisms, ramadan fasting, christmas without jesus, easter without jesus, thanksgiving without native americans. a ship named jesus.

the color of soul is polka dot or striped pimp suit, or red clay or mississippi god damn black, or prince purple, or cherry moon or harlem high yellow, or freckled cherokee, or orange sari, or nina's blues, or miles green or white tongued house negro, or detroit read. dubois, how does it feel to be a problem? a complex idea, malcolm? harriet? sonia? amiri? martin? assata? mumia? black women? native daughter? goddess? fairy? prophet? how does it feel to be a troubled soul. a soul who recognizes the foreign soil searching for safety between our feet. a soul who has known rivers, and mountains, and snow, and rainforests, and cotton, and ritual, and gold, and survival and love.

souls that sometimes forget these are not our eyes. vision impaired
souls who struggle to find their reflection in a looking glass,
breaking with every memory,
every blink of a revelation.
blowing inside the breath of sea-man flagships of the 1400's.
a soul searching for position. a simple human body to house greatness.
a soul asking for it's own soul back.
a color without color or definition or boxes
to put untamed revolutionary souls in.
and you know i got
and you know we got

soul.

love is not the enemy
manifesto for 2008
written sunday, january 27, 2008

all my new boyfriends
are scheduled for 2009.

no more lions in my bedroom.

king is the most important thing in my life

i'm married to my art, my life, my work.

grown-ups are over-rated.

my wonder woman cape never needs to be ironed, even in detroit.

skinny is the new thick.

jessica worship required

(insecure niggas need not apply)

joy is reality.

evil is an illusion.

the devil never wins.

i'm one of god's favorite children &
i have lots of brothers and sisters.

scorpios are misunderstood and not to be
fucked with.

i'm really into my bows and arrows.
in search of a new bow.

mine was broken, along with my heart
in a fist fight with a fallen angel.

love is not the enemy.

i have dream catchers for arms.

why would the person having an affair with my husband have my pictures and pictures of my child (without my permission) all over their myspace page with music he wrote in our home in atlanta playing in the background?

i had to ask. it makes me laugh, actually.

we need to talk about mental illness in
the black community.

am i crazy because i don't expect my son to be forgotten
just because it "happens all the time?"

my name is jessica care moore.

i've been a simmons.

i've been a poole.

i will die a moore.
ain't giving my name away no more.

he would have to fly down from the heavens on an eagle!!!

eagles are becoming extinct, right?

2008 is all about pushing out new work, new ideas, new writing.

2007 sucked. ask anyone.

except watching my son really walk for the first time
on my birthday.

and listening to him to say "yeah" and "hi" and "apple"

he made last year worth not giving up on this year.

2008.

year of the great.

i can't wait.

blessed for my new Ray of sun
blessed for my Wil that helps me fight

grateful all the time to my friends and family

this is the year of completion.

i will pray my way out of confusion.

i will not answer questions i don't want to answer.

i will not speak evil into existence.

i am a love festival.
an international love conference
a multi-media love exhibition
a love magnet with refrigerators, stoves and washing
machines chasing after me as i walk down
woodward avenue.

no one can stop what god
has in store for us.

omari turns 13 this year!!!

time is a trick to keep us on time.

i've fallen back in love with walking.

i'm a cherokee. african. canadian. american.

high yella black girl

from the "d"

building a nest with snowballs, poems &
my one year old's imagination.

won't you dance with me barefoot in the cold?

how many times you gon' play that alicia keys
lesson learned cut with john mayer, mommy!!?

till i get my lesson, baby.

"falling down ain't falling down if you don't cry
when you hit the floor."

so now i'm up. i'm armed. i'm ready.
i'm on my prayer mat.

no patience for callow conversations.

here comes the sun.
here comes my son.

i've never known love like this.

this is the best of me.
and i'm getting better

2008.
year of the great discovery!!!

check your mirror.
always watch your back.
don't let snakes in your home
unless you want snake/pits.

do background checks.

find an infinite line that will return
your heart safely

and draw it with a red wax crayon.

an indelible scar.

unharmed. unshaken. unimpressed.

 a detroit butterfly.

reborn. renamed.
into so many of me.

2008
year of the chosen people
year of the free

love

is not the enemy.

haiku.

no romance without the finance

first of the month came
and went like love often does.
pockets broke n heart

detroit.

malcolm used to be
a black red-haired man. motown.
hand claps in his speech.

he is hip hop.

middle of the month
he jus comes. cramping my style
in a b-boy stance.

Who am I?

i am an native american black girl.

i do not speak portugese
but when i'm in bahia.
i am a brazilada.
not an americana.
i walk the favellas and blend
with the amazon river.

i am an american brown girl poet.
so when i whisper "go papi"
it's also to remind you that not just
puerto rican girls carry knives.

i grew up on fried chicken
but taught myself how to make tofu
taste like   something!!

i can cut banana for cereal
 and fry sweet plantain.

i am a midwest baby.
i wear corn rolls, perm it straight
and even lock it up.

i speak thousands of languages with
just one facial expression.

i was raised on "get your lesson."
i cross my fingers in confession.

i am a muslim in morocco.
a revolutionary "colored" in
south Africa.

i am the anti-exotic

who can cook with the curry
spices of south east asia.

build an hindu inspired alter
with african influences.

and shoot a jumper better than
my brothers.

i am namo before
what's love got to do with it.

i am the spine of the movement
i am the struggle.
i hold secrets. i am the truth.
i am your reflection
your mother u will eventually

marry.

i am mary.
black madonna
hetsepshut
tara
sheba
keisha
tamika

and

kenya

i am the exotic anti exotic
that can outrun you to the corner.
i am a native daughter

and you can only love me
when you learn to
love yourself.

om namo narayani
om namo narayani

rocks bricks and my beautiful stone

I was built to be hard growing up in Detroit. A little girl of steel.
I armed myself with words, but never found the metal durable enough to protect my heart.
I moved back to Detroit to find peace, to collect things, to write and allow my son to be around my family while he was still a baby. I've watched him eventually learn how to say "nana," "uncle mark" "uncle jonny" and "auntie Lisa.," and "auntie Charlotte."

I was hiding the first few months, not wanting to allow people to really know I was back. I didn't know I was back yet. Me and King flew home the end of August 2007, on a ticket from the Museum of African American History. I was the featured poet for a Race Exhibit that was closing. My brother drove a 24 foot truck full of half of my belongings, and met me there the next day. A day later, I was in New Orleans after an invite from Susan Taylor to join Mike Eric Dyson, Hill Harper, Al Sharpton, Angie Stone and others for the 2nd Anniversary of Hurricane Katrina.

Katrina being my legal middle name that has since been lost with "fame" and on books. I felt a connection to that water in a special way. Like New Orleans, I felt like my home was swept away from right under me. I saw the warnings, and I knew a storm was coming, but I didn't move. I was waiting for a sign from God that it was time. A tidal wave.

A hurricane. I thought my son would hold it all together, but, he wasn't even one years old. I remember him wiping the tears from my face and looking so worried about me as an infant.

That's when I knew I had to escape. Return back to the place I started. Sankofa style. To my mom's house, and a few months later my new nest in the center of my city.

The last thing I wanted or was remotely looking for was love, or a "date," whatever that is?? After being married or in relationships for over a decade, I was completely lost in that world.

God has jokes. Yes she does.

I was driving up Jefferson with King talking to a good friend on the phone, when I saw someone I thought I recognized walking up the street. I went past two lights because the long dreadlocks threw me off. My old friend from Wayne State University, I'd maybe seen once since

1993 was a faded up cutie that I'm sure lots of girls had quiet crushes on, me included. He was handsome, laid back.. athletic looking. Always a nice smile. Always cool. Almost seemed shy.

I finally decided to turn around and pulled up to him as he walked. He looked into the car a little puzzled and I quickly apologized, "I'm sorry, I thought you were my old friend ray stone from Wayne State." And he laughed and said, "jessica, I am your friend Ray Stone from Wayne State."

Any good looking man walking in Detroit, on purpose, is rare. He was eating a vegan sandwich. I don't think he really noticed or talked to King much.

My first year back in Detroit changed because of this moment. My son's life was made better because of a simple re-introduction of a familiar face.

God is good.

These poems were inspired by that moment in time. I've realized after two "legal" marriages, that the true commitment we have to find as adults, is the ability to truly be friends. Love people for who they are. Love their faults, their imperfections. We are just people. Rashid El. Ra One. Ray Stone, thank you for your friendship, your wisdom, your support, your inspiration.

You are one of God's favorite children. And will always be one of my favorite people.

> Meet you
>
> in the middle
>
> of the ocean.

the anatomy of a teardrop
november 6, 2007 @ 11:45pm
inspired by rashid el

what is the dna
the chemical make up
the deep algebraic equation

that can break down the
anatomy of a

teardrop.

how much salt equates
how much more pain.

if it falls fast to the
bottom of your nose

and suddenly stops.

what the hell does that mean?

what if you can feel the tear
deep in your gut and you keel
over and feel physically sick
when you try to hold it back.

what if the tear gets stuck
in the corner of one eye.

a stubborn tear that refuses

to fall   for you.

what if the tear is warm like the ocean?
what if the tear is cold as a snowball
crashing into your february face?

what if the tear cut your face
and scarred you for life?

what if the tear turned blood red
when it entered the atmosphere?

an onion tear verses the joy tear

what if the tear refuses to come
when someone dies
or when it's time to say goodbye
to a long time lover?

how many of your tears does it take
to fill a bath that will comfort you?

enable you to wash your hands?

10,000 tears
divided by one heart

equals a whole lot of water.

what if we combined the tears of
little girls molested by their fathers
and uncles?

what if we added up all the tears
washed away in new orleans or indonesia?

the tears of the children of darfur?
south african tears

mothers losing their sons   tears

what about just the tears in this room
or just the tears of the person reading this poem?

would it be enough

to cause the rain to stop
before it hit the ground.

imagine swallowing woodward
after ray stone

imagine swallowing woodward avenue.
the bus stop on Griswold.
the people mover station.
the white guys in loosened ties.
the black women wearing corporate skirts.
union street at lunch.
mason at detroit breakfast house.
the new over-priced markets, opening day at
comerica park, and if only they were closer,
the detroit pistons.

blessed are the poor
who make the rich feel rich.
blessed are the meat eaters
who make the vegetarians thrive.
blessed are those with road rage.
blessed are those who went to
drivers education, to really learn
how to
drive.

blessed are the alleys
fueling the sidewalks ego.
blessed are the hollow
who make the whole feel
full.

blessed are the politicians
who show us they are only people.
flawed, fatherless
a feather in their hat on Sunday.
a dollar in their right hand for the
homeless man & the stripper
on Friday.

imagine birthing a city of people
who walked to work.
who knew the origin of their food.
who didn't feed their babies sugar
and blow blunt smoke in their faces.
imagine if our teenagers got bikes to ride

to school at 16
instead of cars.

imagine side-walk chalk
used for hopscotch
instead of outlining our children
when shot on these paradise valley
streets.

imagine joy road as just that.
imagine herman gardens projects replaced
by basketball courts, new swing sets, batting
cages, a baseball field.
instead of a gate protecting
a mound of dirt.

what if smokey robinson's voice
pushed through the cracks of the cement
when we walked up the boulevard?

what if aretha's franklin's respect,
replaced the pledge of allegiance
in school?

what if the djembe
replaced the school bell?

what if the sound of a baby laughing replaced
the morning prayer.

imagine sea shells as our new iphone.
imagine having to feel the direction
of the wind whenever we traveled.

and imagine having to know how to get
anywhere without "onstar."

imagine living on a blackstar.

imagine if we could find the compass
we were born with.

how we would truly begin to understand the

courage

of the road less traveled.

what if barefoot
was the new jordan shoe?

blessed are the diamonds
that turn back to coal.
blessed are emcees
who sound better
than platinum

but won't ever go   gold.

imagine swallowing detroit whole
in the months that were cold
so when the summer came back
nobody knew it was gone

blessed are men who know
how to make a woman laugh
blessed are the boys
who grow up with their dads.

blessed are the daughters
who get to be little girls.

imagine swallowing woodward
and giving birth to this world.

untitled detroit poem #603
march 24, 2008

lavender in my window
takes the edge off the alley
brick and smells and
woodward avenue
ghosts
protecting this sacred space.
rust colored concrete floors
camouflaged as desert
snow disguised as sun drops.

i am warm despite the cold
of what's supposed to be

spring.

it's so quiet without king
riding his train or asking
for apples.

i can actually here birds singing
downtown.

learning to write with silence
is not easy.

i need something to be making noise.
if there is nothing to block out
no madness, no attacks on my spirit
then how am i to be inspired?

and then there is you.

a mystery from 14 years ago
somebody i used to know
that i wouldn't recognize
years later just three feet from
my car.

you, with the map to the city
and perhaps even my heart
in your pocket.

i used to think i was from detroit
but i am bumping into new streets
everyday.

learning how to drive and walk
around this motor city i became
a woman in
this place,
and now i am
a little girl   doing cartwheels

up the riverwalk.

discovering my home again
across the
street from my canadian family.

my first black eye i wear
like a charm around my neck.

proud, that i look so tough
a mayweather butterfly
a cody high school graduate
a wayne state revolutionary
and even more beautiful

a single mommy

with eight arms and no time
to write the way i used to write.

still

here i am at 10:35 am negotiating
my book orders
invoices
my third book
my solo theater show
cleaning up my place
kweli coming in town
a night babysitter for king

and of course the one thing i can't
seem to escape

love.

he is…

my used-to-be fireman
that we love to watch climb up fire escapes
and makes my baby king laugh hard.

my friend who was there
when i was overwhelmed and
just needed someone to help
balance

the weight of my groceries
and stress and the humiliation
of needing to apply for food stamps

while quietly teaching my little one
how to go to bed

independently.

life is about small things
and big poems and faith
when there is no faith

and hope when you think
all is lost and ruined

or

life may just be a lavender
plant from eastern market

perched against your window
with little light for survival
and a picture of your grandmother
you've never met
but seen in your sister
lisa's face.

both my grandparents on my daddy's side

died young.

so, how can i not attempt to live
or write or smile in the face
of hate and betrayal.

when i have angels i can touch.
who won't let me walk on a
certain side of the sidewalk
or only feed me fruit from
local farmers

and tickles me like i'm 12.

the smell of a genuine man
is a powerful aromatherapy

for a jaded black girl poet
who just stopped believing in the

possibility of people.

when words become
game
not a tradition
passed down.

words, simply gossip salt
on a table that is set for

one family.

and another invades and
mixes blood and pork salt
inside a future soup destined to
be

vegetarian

holistic

blessed.

protected by a place.
a political idea.
a southern promise.
my daddy's cement trucks.

my mom's inability to not work.
my son's eyes.
the romance of afternoon tea
matching laptops and
still dropping it like it's hot
when u are 35 and up.

today i stand up and sometimes i

just dance

for every ancestor
that raised me.

taught me
how to tell my story
and to always be proud
of who and where i was

fearlessly.

with lavender blowing through
my heat vents

and a feather stone in my pocket.

getting a two step
closer to the woman

i was destined
to be.

dear ancient black man in detroit
(an open letter from a native daughter born in the d)

sometimes i cannot write in
this slave language
so i cry

until i find a poem.

having to explain yourself when your
native tongue has been buried under
ancient mounds
and hidden inside the pages of
the hopi book of stars
for centuries
makes it difficult.

how do i begin to know
how to love u?

displaced and taught nothing
about your royalty
your chi
has become an animated video game
a caricature of your true self
programmed to get a job
and live the american dream
that was stolen while u were sleeping.

i almost didn't recognize you
in this life
you have become more stubborn
than your great great great-grandfather
who loved to eat cherries
and ruled centuries before these new libraries
would ever acknowledge.

how did we end up here?

in detroit?
new york city?
morroco?
ethiopia?
atlanta?

monthly
i fight against the sharp piercing of
my warrior blood

forced to spill every 28 days
so that my children can be born

free.

sometimes
i wear coconut oils on my skin
so when u kiss me you will remember
the way i would adorn my feet with henna
and bathe us in rosemary.

the first time i really made salaat
i kneeled down inside a mosque
with a morrocon woman
who only spoke arabic
in marrakech.
i traveled to rabat
algiers
rode a camel through the atlas mountains
washed my body in the face of the
mediterranean sea.

have you forgotten me?

my name is jessica/yasmine/hetsepshut/sheba/fatimah

i've hidden inside the skin
of the hindu goddess tara
oya is my sister
and the sun comes up
when i press play on my ribs
they say you gave me

life.

you were never a slave
you were not born to be their paid gladiators
you have mistaken adultery for polygamy
my love/for a 401k plan

& your need to travel to jupiter,
excavate the moon, see the four corners
live off the beach
and ride across the country by train.

is as beautiful as your spirit.

just survive baby
and make it back home to me.

the quiet revolutionary place
where i just need you
and a half-dozen fresh sunflowers
an etta james record and the taste
of fresh mango pulled from your
smart sweet mouth

native american black man.

i am the yamasse mother of the cherokee,
seminoles, choctaw and apalachees.

much more than a georiga peach
with 30 foot arms and miles of legs
you call branches & mistake for

trees.

my green afro that sheds in the fall
and sometimes turn red as my cousins
cheeks.

i want to tell you i've walked along the
paved streets of cordova

uninterrupted.
gardens grew as i walked
before the lie of europe was born.

i am the birthplace of the atlantic, euphrates
and named the great lakes
you often visit in solace or sometimes
feel when we shower after making love.

there is a reason you sing, you know?

i used to paint you in scarlet and
drape you in the sweet gold
of the sun.

this morning i only wish to boil water
for fresh peppermint tea
and wait for you to
simply   smile.

as the pain of confusion and the ongoing
search for sovereignty over your own
existence
takes over your attempts to live proud
in this nation that taught you

to keep your head down and turn
against your own people, your history.

i built you a place of worship
in the middle of our kitchen and fed our children
couscous and apples.
planted rubber trees in our backyard
with seeds i sprouted and saved in my hair
while singing chushite lullabies
to our future seeds.

i am your reflection

always growing
always choosing.

i'm sorry i only speak in poems
it's the only language that understands
what i'm trying to say...

i am the girl you run away with
not the woman you have to leave behind
to become a
man.

i am the underground railroad
with a 360 degree track
the runaway slave with a map
and the one that never felt a chain
or a whip
i build pyramids in south america, georgia,
mexico and egypt.

i am the spoon.
there is no spoon.

(sometimes i just wanna spoon)

i created sand storms in the sahara
to get your attention.
blew smoke shaped ohms through
a wood pipe to warn you the
rain was coming.

i was there before they say i was there
i am the invisible woman
the black queen that sat by the door
the bluest eye
the diary of eagles

a daughter's geography
the best local beer in any bar in america.

and sometimes i am just a black girl
hiding her divinity
under a baseball cap
and a nice jump shot
on the westside of detroit
hoping you will recognize my skills
when the wind is still
and the fish are swimming
upstream
and there is less noise & distraction
so many years later
back to that ancient place
where we forgot to fall in love
with no broom to jump
and the vow was only to live
long enough to find

each/other/again

in this desert named detroit
swallowed up by potholes and
abandoned pyramids.

still searching for our future
walking up a serendipitous busy city street
our ancestors hoping we will understand
that this time the hello
may be more than a promise.

it could possibly be your gift

and i didn't call your beeper number
over a decade ago because i understood

that god makes no mistakes
and our tables are already set

& sometimes a kiss from truth
can change the world.

it's so much deeper than getting wet

so kiss my ancient hurricane mouth
like we haven't met

yet.

JELLO

nas said:
"god love us thug niggas
cause next to jesus on the cross
was the hood nigga..will he forgive us?"

it's not that i don't love
jello. i love jello. i ate so
much red #5 pork jello when
i was pregnant. something about
it.

it's not that i didn't watch
the cosby show.

we all watched the cosby show.
whether you were poor or middle
class or didn't have a tv

somehow we found a way to catch
this affluent black family on network tv
on thursday nights.

the first since good times
with any real impact that i can
remember.

i loved denise. she was a weirdo
like all yellow black girls who
weren't quite ghetto enough to
be down with black girls at

public school.

but just enough swagger to
land the cute boys and find a
way to make your "difference"
a

fashion statement.

i love the classics with bill
and richard pryor.

his comedy is classic.
i cried when he lost his son.

i just don't understand the
constant attack against poor

black people in this country
without the balance of why

why are we here. why we are going

back/ward.

as this country continues to
to vote for our civil rights.

we/the removed/black africans/native people/
before the slave ship

with our comfortable cul de sac
lives.

our nannies and gardeners and
private schools—to keep their
children away from the rift raft.

our tinted windows that loathe
our own babies
scared of our own children.

we speak of black men and young
black girls as if we aren't their

mommas & daddies.

i know there is work to be done.

i also know there is a reason why
crack was created/distributed and
sold to my community.

i understand that nooses have never gone
out of style.

just repackaged/commodified/and incorporated.

that we are born into a poverty
in our minds

passed down from generation to generation

i grew up knowing that if the hot
water is cut off.

you just boil water. and you present
yourself to the world the same way
you would on any morning.

you iron your clothes
and you keep you head up

we are a people of pride and tradition
we are not just baby mama's and titty
dancers.

and we are that too.

we are dysfunctional families.
we live in a dysfunctional country.

still.

we must teach our children
up from slavery.

we must teach our children
without their books
if there are books at all.

we must start from a place of
love and history
not disdain and disgust.
we must start from a place of
revolution and self empowerment
not humiliation & finger pointing.
i challenge the black middle/lower/upper class
to give back to the poor neighborhoods
they were born into.
more than a speech
more than a nasty look
when they drive past the hood and see
young boys with pants hanging lower
than you'll ever understand.

i challenge you to offer a belt
heavier than the chains of slavery
to hold an entire people up
by the waist
cut us down from the tree
and teach us how to truly be

free.

Mike Vick

American Villain

When I met Mike Vick we were both checking into a Delta flight in Atlanta. It was about 7am, and I was in a rush. He was on crutches and had people bringing his boxes of shoes out of a car. We both had corn rolls. I didn't recognize him. I'm more of basketball fan, but I liked Mike Vick when he was the Quarterback for the Atlanta Falcons. He reminded me of the way Barry Sanders ran with the Lions. He was standing around and I jumped in front of him and asked the Delta Rep to check me in, as I had a flight I needed to catch. He looked at me puzzled, but I think he liked the way I didn't know him at that moment. I never imagined the world knowing him for something other than the game of football.

This is for him.

one of janet jackson's tits
stopped america
from the luxury of their
pork and beer and family hour
of football on primetime television.

a quick glimpse of this natural dark phenomenon
shook the fat white beer bellies and right wing
like a juicy piece of bbq
dripping like blood
covering the carpets of america's
brutal living/dead room that powers it's
brains with their tv god

teaching us that a woman's body is not sacred.
one brown breast exposed for two seconds
is a sin in this home of
puritans and pilgrims

while we are forced to watch and smell them
bloated, pierced, hairy, funky
beer bellies of men who have five tits
to our two
sweating profusely as they scream at their favorite
football team
shoving cheetos down their throats

acting as if their children really give a damn who wins.

football is an outside sport.

when's the last time any of you went outside and threw the pig skin?

played under the sun and the stars?
it is a violent game   that paralyzes.
excites the gladiator in us.

all this superbowl attention to a single
black quarter back and the fighting of pit bulls

but what about the abused wives of players?

what is the fine for beating your wife
after a bad loss?

are we ready to ruuuumble?

young man. rumble.

they rape women they rape dogs..

we live in a country that used to muzzle african women
and rape them like wild animals
fight enslaved shackled african men
gladiator style

and mike vick is the villain?

let's be clear. i'm an animal lover. i cried when
i had to leave my dog crystal behind when my mom
left my daddy. he was a mut and crazy as hell. nobody
would ever wanna fight crystal. he was part poodle and dug up
the damn yard like a hound dog. but around the block we knew
some fools who fought the pits and we weren't allowed to go. it
was a part of the culture of the neighborhood.

dog fighting
chicken fighting
slaves fighting

violent contact sports

boxing
football

hockey

american as apple pie.

you can lose
your legs. your game. your teeth. your life.
your legs. your game. your teeth. your life.

your career.

especially if you are a talented
fast quarter back

and

black

in the NFL.

black/south/africa

when i traveled to south africa for the first time
i met a wonderful artist...a german/jewish
sculptor susan woolf who gave out oranges to black
south africans on the street and told me
and my traveling partner, val, stories about
her family being tied up and robbed in their
own home.

still, this artist who had been commissioned for large work
in banks and museums, kept her modest studio in the hood.

she had a large body of work with local south african
tea bags she collected and people offered.
each bag represented the necessity for housing.

each conversation i had. every experience on the southern tip
of africa changed the way i thought about life in america
in some way.

one of the moments that stays with me is the young jewish daughter
who found a copy of my first book in her house and ate it in one night.

she was waiting to speak to me the next morning. full from a lot of
black nationalist ideas and quite perplexed about what/who i was
in the guest room of her family's house.

she wanted to know why i felt i had to carry the burden of my blackness
and wanted me to know i was lucky to have been born in america. i
would never had been able to write and speak about the same things
under apartheid rule.

georgia
alabama soweto
mississippi soweto
jim crow
race riots
detroit chicago little rock

she didn't realize that

lynching

was an

international

sport.

personal vocabulary
(for the Caversham Arts Centre, Durban, South Africa)

Foreign/to consider myself/foreign
In the home of my ancestors.
Misplaced child of Africa
Cutting my hands on the barbed wire.
Separating oceans and ideas and language.
My split tongue searching for Zulu
As Elizabeth serves tea and wonders
Why these black girls don't understand.

It is difficult to explain ourselves.
How the landless American-Africans share
Eyes and clothes-lined stories
Washed clean and hung to dry
In this season of black frost.

Cold realities ground us.
Our fathers buried in the same red clay
As U.S. apartheid quietly segregates our
Integrated schools, neighborhoods and bookstores.
Mud brick shanty homes line the streets of Detroit
Georgia, Ohio, Chicago, East New York.

Mud brick people living in concrete jungles.
Displacement upon displacement.

How have I become tourist? On safari?
My arms stretch and curve like baobab trees.
Wind blown and frozen in place
Crying out to the heavens.
Crushed duality stains my palms with
Fresh mint leaves   sweet
As Vusumuzi's smile.
The eldest of his house

I think of my brothers, father(s).
Of my own family's vocabulary filled with silence
Inherited from my mother(s).
Forcing me to question the world
Outside our comfortable three floor
Red brick house.
My identity formed around a spirit
In my head/beneath the surface of my skin.
Negro bones never quite giving into the

Joints or curves or circles.
Life will insist you run
Far away from your roots.
So you can never find your destiny
Chiseled inside the bone of your cheek.
I cover my head and wrap my body
Inside a white hijab.
I figure the only place that can be
Saved from colonization must be hidden.
Swallowed, whole.
Pretend you are not smart.
Don't speak in tongues out-loud.
Your brain may cover gallery walls.
Your canvas, splattered with fish oils
And water paints
To fill your tank and poison the air
For 1.65 per gallon.

What does this have to do with South Africa
Western   you   ???
Never prayed or listened in that direction.
You/holocaust survivor/yes
My great-great grandmother

Swam/sank/shackled   against the ocean.
I fly 18 hours
& complain about   the space
in coach/a graveyard drowning
in it's own history

                below.
.
Outside my window at Caversham Centre
Butterflies find love.
The only thing that is sure to save us
And kill us all at once
Depending on what you love and
What you are willing to die for.
Some will say you are a violent   savage.
Others will ordain you revolutionary
And print your face on silk screened t-shirts

Complex as advanced calculus.
Simple as a sunset or locating mars.

How you see it

depends on
Which direction you are standing.
Or if you are standing at all
When the tide rises up
An army of ocean people
Asking for soldiers for a

Century old fire.

Will you hide behind your Western Education?
Meditate the gun in the other direction with your
Eastern Religions?

Which land is truly foreign?
Which land bears your blood?
Is it arrogant to feel entitled?

Un-taxable?

I think of the genocide of my Native American ancestors
The 1920's rural south racism my prideful daddy was born into
His move up north hoping to find freedom and work
His rifles that protected our home during the riots

I guess I've always felt foreign/a stranger
To my own mirror/my own country
A romantic in search of my ancestral birth mother
The place where the middle is merely a place
Where I   begin
The passage, fluid, without spiritual death
Or acceptance of a new name.

No slavery.

The word eradicated from existence.
The idea itself, an abomination.
Perhaps I am taking this too personal.
The nightmare of being separated by
Hair, Skin and Nail tests
Keeps me up at night.

Writing poems by candlelight.
Peeling back the bitter skin of words
To find new meaning inside a passion fruit.
A personal vocabulary
Only mastered when free.

for the children of gaza

(from God is Not an American, solo show.
NYC Opening, Apollo Theater 2009)

I have no windows. No doors in my home.
My neighborhood, sports clubs, schools, hospitals, are now
targets for artillery shells.

Only a generator to keep me connected to the outside
World. Remember when wars had rules?

Remember when you could find our land
On a map?

These drones do not see us as people.
Our children are not their children.

Their small bodies scattered on the street, like
Torn pieces of paper from a headline.
Empty words and no truth about their
Story attached to tiny limbs blown
off.

Fingers, arms, teenage bodies cut in half
This blood is too new to be spilled. Still
Finding its way, swimming past young, soft bones.

Hundreds killed. Thousands wounded.

Children are told to hide with their families
In schools and then the building is shelled.
Innocence stolen and they are left with this moment
For eternity.
Left alone for days, holding onto the limp
Bodies of their dead mothers.

Asking them to wake up. They want to go home.
But they are home.

What does that mean to the rest of the world.
I wonder?

Is democracy at work?
What are the hours?
9-5pm?
We can't tell the night from day
I think freedom is at lunch

Or taking a Monday off to barbeque.

Today I choke in search of fresh air without
Shrapnel cutting my tongue.

I eat bombs. I tell myself. They cannot kill me.
I think about God. The God everyone claims they pray to.
Where is God now? Sitting on the North Star?
Invading another country as a distraction?
Hiding inside
A rocket launcher
Blowing up a Mosque?

Murder in the name of God.

What is closer to God
Then children laughing?

Maybe we should begin praying to that sound?

I suppose there were bombs in their lunch boxes
As they attempted normalcy
By still walking to school.

Or the sisters who were burnt to death
In their sleep.

The fireworks are death lights here with no
Musical score.

My friend says he hopes if he is killed,
His children are killed so they won't be
Suffering inside this massacre of this attack
On civilian life
alone.

We understand Toni Morrison. Beloved are the women
Who take their children with them. Jump off sides
Of ships. Rooftops.

To hear a father talk this way…

Anything, but pain and death
as a way of life.

One of the Israeli Missiles screams out

"We are not the enemy!"
Then tore through the body of a pregnant woman
of two Palestinian boys.

Their mothers promised them change. Now velvet
blood And prayer beads.
Cover their mouths and hands.
They died with Allah in their heart.
And their hands toward the sun.

This is not new news. If news at all.

The f16 choppers attacks homes with
20 missiles in less than 5 minutes.

Soldiers march inside my mouth
Slide down my throat
Crawl inside my womb
And leave a hand grenade.

So I will feel this war as a birth.
But of what?
Of blood?
Of children's bones?
Of decapitation?
Of hate?
Of geography?

Occupation always produces violence.
But I am asked to speak of peace.

How can I with bombs exploding
killing the unborn
And their siblings?

Why is genocide acceptable?
To some people
& not to others?

Holocaust verses holocaust verses holocaust.

The ones they celebrate.
The ones they never mention.

I feel as if I am burnt to ash.
My shoes being thrown into a pile of others shoes

My ancestors ripped from their homeland and
Sold like cattle.

The place with God on their money
Are they going to save me now?

Where is America?
In a series of long meetings.
Mourning the loss of the family cat?

There is no place for politics in the
Face of genocide. But genocide is
political.
religious.

How much money to clean the blood off
the streets of DC, Texas, Ohio, Baltimore
We already dead. They think. Still, we fight without
Armor.

Our children's dead flesh becomes our skin.
We wear the mask. Attempt smiles.

I don't jump as much
When I hear them. Coming. Falling. Right on my block.
I just hold onto to an object, and shake inside and wait for it to be over.

It is never over.
It is freezing cold. I dream of summer. I dream of
Warm food and a hot shower. I dream of freedom.

In Chicago. In Detroit. In Harlem. In Brooklyn. In Soweto.
In Compton. In Oklahoma. In Kansas. In Cuba. In Gaza.

End Apartheid
In South Africa. In Alabama. In our education system. In our
Subconscious. In Dearborn. In Mississippi. In our judicial system.
In our prisons.

In our policies. In our death chambers. In our mind.

End apartheid

In Gaza

Our mosques. Our homes. Destroyed.

In Gaza

Some of our own sit in silence.

In Gaza.

There is no electricity

In Palestine.

There is no water.

Where there is no water, There is no life.

I scrape the blackness of this night/sky on fire
And wrap it around myself for shelter.

Tomorrow I will find a cloud for my head.
And I will summon a light rain to shower.

God is close. God is coming.
Between our breath
Before another bomb calls our name

We will answer back.
We will sit in one room.
If we die. We die together.
No one will be left behind.
This is bravery of God's people.

We will not cower beneath the rubble of
A Rafah Refugee Camp.

We will scream.
We will pray
Injustice in
the other direction.

We will find peace
In death
If not in
life.

Amen.

I took out the garbage
poem before 2009.

i took out the garbage.

2 bags.

i wore your favorite silver/gray dickie zip up.

i made two trips.

the first one was cold.

there was a black and white one way street sign

stuck in the snow

next to the big bin full of stuff
connected perpendicular
to blue and white street names

comstock and conant.

i'm still learning the east/side.

i took it. i like it.

there are gifts everywhere.

the second trip, with the second bag

wasn't so bad.

i skipped across the hills like a little girl.
i stomped my pink boots inside the snow

to try to remember

when this was a season
i used to have fun inside.

just like our season together

it was a very

good

year.

dhs office trip #7

the homeless man gives my son a dollar.
i am hiding.
hoping to not look like i'm doing
well.
doing well doesn't
go with the chairs at this office.

i am thankful and embarrassed.

the same day i was booked for a show in paris,
asked to be in a film being shot in harlem in the summer
and booked for a keynote at another college.

my son's health insurance was cancelled by the state.
and the daycare said i owe them three grand and i
have to pay it so my son can register
for the new year.

the daycare lady is asking me if i have a job

again.

i am a famous, recognized poet and writer.
i have performed in south africa.
i am an apollo legend.

remember me?

i was on the cover of the metro times last month?
the cover of african american family when my son
began here in the summer. his pic on the inside.

my photos are in full color and six feet tall at
the museum of african american history.
i am one of the women of a new tribe.

i am on exhibit, on display.

always, on display.

exactly what does being a legend pay?
i need some w2's for this life

king's father says he wants a dna test.
i'm told my son is apparently from an
affair with a rapper
i used to love…
so why am i calling
you for
winter sweaters?
of course
he only speaks this way
when he has an audience

this is madness, i tell myself.

in order to receive help from the state
you have to be working.

my writing is my work. i can't have my
son 24 hours a day and write and create

new work.

question marks float on top of the head
of the case workers?

herbie hancock plays in the background
this is the music i brought into this place.

never leave your music at home.
never leave your music at home.

they only play the tv on one station
in the lobby
the sci fi channel or something.

sometimes there are cookies full
of m&m's

king, don't touch the cookies baby.

i made up a job because my job is not a job
i made up a job because my job is not a job

and apparently told them i made too much money
that doesn't really exist.

so now i will be allocated twelve dollars
a month for food.

my 1st husband calls me by mistake.
in the middle of all this..

we laugh about reading poems for
20 years.
our son. my earth son cracks jokes
about him getting old.

we are elders and we still young
says kevin powell.

this is a thankless job, weldon irvine
would whisper in my ear at the
schomberg before he killed himself
a few years later.

thankless.
thankless
thankless

thank you
thank you
thank you

thankless thankless thankless thank you thank you...

joni mitchell to drown out the moment
mariah carey anita baker jennifer hudson
and yeah, even that new beyonce song.

if i were a boy.

thank you

angels past lovers ex-husbands
rappers dj's producer's basketball
players guitar players novelists
philosophers. painters. bulllshiters.

haters. liars. oh. the liars. bless you.

industry intellectuals that will never
get it.

all you deep mutha fuckas

thank you

mos

for telling me it was honorable
to live my life
travel the world

and when people ask what i

do

i simply say

i am a poet.

thank you kweli for being a friend outside the music

thank you roger guenevere smith

for huey and the head nod

to ossie for the elbow in my arm

and that smile

thank you nas for the prediction
cause we never know the outcome

thank you, Last Poets, Sonia,
Haki, and Baraka...

thank you ma nana for buying
coats and uncles for shoes
and daycare.

moore family.

i have more family.

i was born a moor.

i'm headed to la for some shows.

i have to stop crying and write

this show.

this is not a show.
this is my life

god.

this is my life.
this is my life

my blessing
my gift.

gotta gig in nati while i
was writing this.

my january rent

thank you

daddy god past lover's
present lover
got your text baby.
i'm okay.

thankless thankless

thanksgiving
no thank you
said the abused turkeys

no thank you
for your slaughter
in the name of giving
in the name of family

poems

this is what i have to

give.
i'm eating poems today.

i'm thankful
i'm humiliated
i'm embarrassed
i'm surviving

i'm surviving
i'm writing

odetta just died

you can't stop me
no, you can't stop me.

this is my job

dammit.

this is my job. u know?

i am a mother. give me my check.

amen
amen
amen.

a woman.

a poet

thank you
thank you
thank you.

i'm hiding all the turkeys
in my backyard next year.

then how u gonna give thanks?
some gotta die for you to be
thankful?

i miss you
yale
richard pryor
tom moore
miriam makeba

sekou sundiata
weldon irvine
joseph
rosa parks

you can't find them
you can' t find me.

we are busy writing
we are busy confusing
your paperwork with real

life

my lover says he talks to
me in real

life

the internet is an illusion
people addicted to illusions

though?

thankless thankless

world.

not me not me not me not me not me not me not me not me not me
not me not me not me not me not me not me not me not me not me
not me not me not me not me not me not me not me not me not me
not me not me not me not me not me not me not me not me not me
not me not

me.

Barack Obama
& the State of Black Women in Love

For my mother who said after over 40 years of resistance, and the heartbreak of the 60's riots, Kennedy and King assassinations, she would finally consider becoming an American so she could vote for Barack Obama.

It's difficult to have a love affair with your country.
When you've been portrayed as it's mammy.
The caretaker of the country's children, but not the woman
                    of the house.

A house built with your ancestors' hands
Painted white and shadowed by blood stained windows.
A peculiar institution with your body as witness
Classrooms of misinformation running as the bell rings
Under your armpits
Through your nostrils
Out your throat
Between your toes.

The birthplace of dance.
Jazz. Tap. Hip Hop.

Your native feet never needed to be discovered.
They were already connected to a place. This land
is your land. This land was already my land.

I carry a red and blue earth friendly tote
With the words HOPE written in white
To hold my son's diapers now.

This is peculiar for me.

A few years ago, someone, a fellow poet, a friend,
An activist would've asked.

Why so patriotic, jess?

It's naïve to think the revolution has arrived
That all is well!
Children are being bombed
In Palestine
As I write this poem.

It is still a revolutionary act
to simply love.
To hope?
I don't want to die and leave my son
Fiery words & no peace.

Don't want him to rewrite the same poems
In my same voice
thirty years after my work is considered the
past.

The same way they say our writing sounds like
The Black Arts Movement.
Because not much has
moved in this country.

Has it?

Since Jim Crow on the Race Riots or
Facebook or Myspace or Amadou or
The Jena 6.

Until now, maybe.

I watch the pearls around Michelle's neck
I imagine them as cowry shells
She is long and regal and beautiful and brown.
Tall as Mausi Women painted red.
I know President Barack Obama sees this
and this makes me love
the idea of him.

Even more.

Him. Kenyan and American rooted.
Knowing himself and loving himself enough
to not be swayed by Harvard so much.
That he would forget what he would really
need grassroots activism and a comrade
who loved him

To get him to a higher place.

She is more than our generation's Jackie O.
An unapologetically brilliant woman with daughters

as wings
& husband as Chief.

This is a new American story
I am not ashamed to pass down.

For the first time, I am inspired to imagine
The possibility of an Inaugural poem.

I am too revolutionary, I am told. Perhaps?
But, I don't listen to those words.

I have lived my life in the triality
of many Americas.
As Native. As Ancestor. Mother. Pioneer. Griot.
Warrior. Holder of secrets. Lover. International
Representative. Cook.

Who better than the daughters of Harriet and Ida
Coretta and Betty?
Phyllis and Billie?

Someone might have told a young Obama
His life wasn't possible.

So, how can I not imagine a poem?

I'm sure Michelle wasn't
always confident she would find a loyal
man to share her life with.
None of this is certain. And it doesn't matter
Who does read the poem that day..

But wouldn't it be perfect in the ancestral air of sonia?
Or the grace of   ruby
The blues of   jayne.
The hurricane of   asha.
The imagery of   pearl
The spitfire of   nikkey

???

Who better to write about it
& tell the world about
How we feel?

About the image of those beautiful smiling girls
in pigtails and twists as their mom and
their dad enter a sacred space
many of us had written off as impossible.
or hoped for in our
grandchildren's lifetime.

Not today.

Being inspired to even consider writing
a poem, a homage for an American
President and his family in my lifetime.
Has shown me the possibility of what can
truly be manifested beyond dreams.

I am told today that the moon aligned itself
With Jupiter and Uranus and it won't happen again
until 2052.

I believe that life & exact science & astrology can be
altered when God decides to make it so.
And while many are celebrating a first
in America's History

I am quietly chanting

Welcome Home.
Welcome Home Barack
Welcome Home Michelle
Welcome back those at War.
Welcome Back to America.

Langston's America.
El Hajj Malik Shabazz's America.
Martin's Dream of America
My blue collar mother and
cement laying daddy's
America.

We have work to do.
And many things to
Un/do.
In the midst of so many uncertain days
In this place called America.

And like so many women in love.
At times I still thought I was alone
Days after the inauguration
At awkward moments
Tears would just come..
While watching the news.
Seeing that mall.
Watching them dance
After hearing my 2 year old, King scream
"Obaaaaaama!"

Until I began asking other women
Many of them single moms..
In private, they say, yes!
It is happening to them too.

Perhaps he is the father
of a New America.

?

I know I feel the heart of this
Country beating again.
Just enough life & breath and hope
To make our historical blues
seem less in vain.

As the night essence of white stars
Finally fall
        Touching the ground

And finding the hearts of

Women

Of men
Of children

Of we

the people.

Letter to self. *(Final)*
Detroit: November 17, 2008

this letter is not for every woman, but maybe, just maybe, you!

dear jess,

after a decade of marriage and a nearly yearlong relationship with a
beautiful friend, i have to write myself this letter as a promise. i
hope it's a promise that other women like me will make to themselves.

when u have been forced…

to spend your life fighting against the often aggressive sexual
exploitation of women through institutions, laws, the workforce, your
own family, school and just basic can't walk down the street without
being harassed your whole life….

when u are a woman of color, and you have survived being stereotyped
as every "round the way girl" at a bus stop, every video stripper in
every rapper's video."

if you have decided, despite your family not coming from a line of
doctors, lawyers or educators, to take your own life, your story, your
fucking destiny into your own hands.

i am asking. no, i am daring you to be courageous enough.
to be fearless and confident enough….

when u have found a way to build an independent economic empire of
your own..

when u told your nine to five to kiss your ass and told your family
to deal with it.

the moment after you decide to no longer be a slave.

when you decide to not believe that the only thing you have to look
forward to in life is making babies and being a wife.

when u find a way to delicately balance babies, be a wife and still
find time for a long bath at least one night per week.

when u have vowed to raise daughters as warriors.

and grown out your perm, or read more books than what would ever be required in school.

when u decide to write your own relevant story and not wait for validation from a culture outside of your own.

from no one!

when u survive on paint, and words, education, and activism, and love and poetry and theater, sewing needles, fabric, real films, and dance and music not always played on the radio.

when u decide, despite the guns at your head.
to outlive your circumstance...
and breathe down the throats of those
who say you don't matter.

when u have done all this.

and a man or a woman that you love tells you that
they feel inadequate. insecure. not quite enough.
not good enough.

around you. or you make them feel less than what they are.

they feel emasculated.

because you are so together, so strong, so perfect to
bring around their mommas.

i am telling you to never say

"no you're not baby." "you have lots of potential"

or make excuses because you are afraid of being alone, or "who's gonna want to marry me with three kids?"

or decide you better tone done your mouth so he won't be scared of you.

when people pay you to talk!

if you have already become a cul de sac clone to fit it with the rest of the women in the neighborhood.

when you have had to pay to get your last name back at least once already when you weren't the one cheating!

never say, to this magical, dreamy person that you love.

"you are perfect for me, i don't care how much money you make or the car you drive." even if u don't care, don't tell them that.

you know what i want you to say.

what i dare you to say fierce bad ass bitch.

you say.

you know what.

you are inadequate.

and i don't date potential anymore

that is so 85!

and i am waaaay too fabulous for you.

you're right!!!

what in the hell was i thinking!!

you say that.

and i promise you

like i'm promising myself

you will do something extraordinary

that day.

it will change your life.

and even if u eventually give in

and decide, like most women

to settle for less than what they are

or what they deserve.

at least you will have that one day

when u realize
that you were born
with everyone you need to survive
on this planet.

and as much as everyone knows how

much i am in love with love.

there is no greater love, then the
one u have with your creator and
yourself.

when u truly decide to not entertain

mediocre, inferior beings

who will only suck everything creative

out of your body.

you will get rid of those fibroids
from stress.

and instead of crying because you are
so powerful and magnificent and you
haven't found a king

who can handle your light

just yet..

you will write your first screenplay
choreograph a work of art
complete your strongest piece of prose
become the ceo of your own company
get that tenure u deserve
teach your girls how to love themselves
inspire someone to buy a book
compose a symphony
write a best selling novel

apply for that grant
raise your sons alone

build an institution

a safehouse!!

for strong, incredible women

who don't have to pretend to not be

well read, articulate, brilliant, talented, soulful,

and fine as hell.

when we know we are.

and so do they.

you will be too busy taping this shit to
your fridge

or emailing it to his inbox

and smiling and exploding with

joy!!!

all my love,

jessica care moore

Jessica Care Moore is a source, a spiritual force, the obeah, and the conjurer of cultural memories. Descending from lineage of poet-warriors and culture-bearers from Africa, England, America, Alabama and Detroit, Moore utilizes the power of the word to condense the social construction of isms that separate the self from the communal. In the labyrinth of Moore's prose and poetry, the blues force is synonymous with the Derridean trace in the way in which the language transverses celestial realms to reclaim or to re-contextualize God in an image that does not reflect the sensibilities and patriarchal attitudes of the Western world. *God Is Not An American* summons the spirits of the androgynous Gods written out of theological and scholarly texts. The book depicts the complexities of God.

In the text, Moore performs ritual and praise song to African and Native American deities of love, beauty, intimacy, fertility and motherhood that have been sacrificed for the Gods of War and Power. Moreover, Moore's poetry serves as libation to her ancestors of Native American, African, and English descent whose blood is the mortar that has built the foundation of America but has been largely trivialized or ignored by the dominant culture. Hence, God is not an American and will not become an American until America wholeheartedly embraces the amalgamation of cultures that have contributed to her work.

With her latest collection of poetry, *God Is Not An American*, Jessica Care Moore has ascended to a new zenith in her career as a professional poet. Similar to Ralph Ellison's *Invisible Man* and Gayl Jones *Corregidora*, Moore's fuses cultural memory, black American musicality and traditional African American literary traditions to broaden the parameters of contemporary black poetry. Influenced by the poets of the Black Arts Movement such as Sonia Sanchez, Nikki Giovanni, Jayne Cortez, Amiri Baraka, and Lucille Clifton, Moore writes mostly in free verse and experiments with musical forms that range from blues, jazz, soul, and hip-hop. The poems in this collection demonstrates Moore's mastery of alliteration, allusion, repetition, metaphor, simile, and internal rhymes that are prevalent in Black American music. In addition, Moore's use of signifying and mascon wordplay further illustrates her ability to transform ancestral wisdom from the economies of slavery and the colonial experience into a truly excellent work of artistry.

Moore's provocative title is by far not an anti-American manifesto, yet in a post-Bush and post-colonial era the book boldly announces the humanity of the quintessential "other" to the Occidental Empires and the oppressive police state nations. *God Is Not An American* centralizes the complexities of the black and colonial experience(s) while simultaneously challenging marginalized and subjugated communities to transcend the boundaries of nationality, sexuality, and race that restrict their humanity. The text calls into question the centuries old limitations placed on individuals who voluntarily and/or forcibly forsake their identity, language, and culture in order to become a citizen (in many cases a second or third class citizen) of the New World. *God Is Not An American* challenges the audience to become socially and politically active in a global community that pacifies "the other" with materialism, consumerism, false hope, and undying thirst for opulence.

In this poetic masterpiece, Moore attempts to spiritually connect the marginalized other to their forgotten past. A time before the European encounter. The poetry affronts the "isms" that are the catalysts of the physical and psychological conditions impacting disenfranchised and people of color. *God Is Not An American* serves as a futuristic point of return. To the casual reader, a futuristic point of the return, is nonsensical term or an oxymoron; however, in many non-western cosmologies a spiritual journey to one's past is vital to the future generation. Time in the Western sense of the word does not exist—there is no separation between the past, present and future.

In several of the poems, Moore builds upon the bildungsroman tradition of African American literature utilizing the journey motif to both physically and spirituality travel across domestic and global spheres in order to negotiate, challenge, and reverse psychological conditions that stem from the colonial experience. For instance, in several of the poems, Moore's hometown Detroit becomes a spiritual oasis, a muse, or a Mecca in which the poet draws wordplay, inspiration, and strength to contest overt and covert institutional racism and sexism. Likewise, the rural landscape of Alabama becomes a sacred space for communal bond, remembrance of the ancestors and the communal memories of love, blind hatred, and legalized terrorism against brown and black bodies. It is important to note, the nostalgia of the past featured *God Is Not An American* remains honest and unsentimental hearkening upon transgressions of the past tempered by racism and sexism to convey to the present and future generations that they "the other" descend from opulent legacy of creators and survivors.

In addition, Moore gives voice to the often silences communities of women subjugated under oppressive, patriarchal systems. Similar to the West African griots, Moore time-binds ancestral wisdom to address the contemporary plights impacting the hip-hop generation by incorporating praise-songs, folktales, and genealogies to establish a connection between past and present. With the wordplay of Sanchez, Clifton, and Giovanni and the style and flamboyance of Josephine Baker,

Moore introduces the audience to African-based worldviews by blending elements of West African and Caribbean religiosity with Islamic and Christian culture to challenge the readers to search for spiritual truth. In the book, Moore engages in sankofic (re) memorization by conjuring up discursive cultural memories of black experiences across the Diaspora. Specifically, Moore weaves the stories of slavery and the testimonies of the colonized with modern parables of survivors and victims of rape, incest, terrorism, police brutality, institutional racism, and white patriarchal socialization.

By far her most personal work, Moore blurs the lines between the introspective and communal struggle. In *God Is Not An American*, Moore delves heavily into the her personal trails and tribulations with self-love, black love, love for community, love for mankind, dysfunctional love, love for the craft of poetry and Godly love. Similar to blues women such as Billie Holliday, Bessie Smith and Gertrude "Ma" Rainey, Moore most intimate moments of pain and passion become the muse for her poetry which articulates the her triumphs with love as well as the loss of her father, loss of childhood friends, the loss of her stepchildren, and divorce. The book highlights Moore's uncanny ability to convey honest depictions of love not overly romanticized with Victorian sensibilities yet not overly morbid or dysfunctional images of love often shown in hip-hop and pop culture. She enables the audience to relate and (re) experience the tragic comedic elements of love experienced by survivors of slavery and/or the colonial encounter. *God Is Not An American* encourages the reader to become God-like by overcoming their conditioning by seeking and becoming true to their individual and universal truths.

Jessie L. Adolph, **Ph.D. Candidate**
English and African Diaspora Studies
University of Missouri-Columbia

about the author

jessica Care moore is an internationally recognized poet, playwright and performance artist. She is the author of three plays, *The Revolutions in the Ladies Room, Alphaphobia* and her new Multi-Media Theater Show, *God is Not an American* which premiered at The Apollo Theater in 2009. She is the CEO of Moore Black Press, and is the author of *The Words Don't Fit in My Mouth, The Alphabet Verses The Ghetto* and *God is Not an American*. She has performed her work all over the world, including South Africa, France, Scotland, Holland and Germany. She is an Apollo Legend and an award winning book publisher. Her house has published Saul Williams, Danny Simmons, asha bandele, Sharrif Simmons, Etan Thomas, and ras baraka.

Her writing has been anthologized by many mainstream publishing houses, and she is proud to be the youngest poet featured in the Prentice Hall's Anthology of African American Women Writers. She is one of the returning stars of *HBO's Russell Simmons Def Poetry,* and Hosted and Executive Produced her own show, *SPOKEN,* directed by Robert Townsend on the Black Family Channel.

Her poetry has been translated into french, japanese and german. She has shared stages and worked closely with many artists, such as, Nas, Sonia Sanchez, Patti Labelle, Cassandra Wilson, Weldon Irvine, Stephanie Mills, Mos Def, Antonio Hart, Marc Cary, Talib Kweli, Gregory Hines, Amiri Baraka, the late Ossie Davis, Ruby Dee, KRS, The Last Poets, Nikki Giovanni, Swiss Chris, Imani Uzuri, Steffanie Christi'an and Ntozake Shange.

She is the proud mother of one beautiful birth son, King Thomas, an earth/son Omari, and three stepchildren, Kelsey, Jaden and Israel.

She is a Detroit Tiger, (*go Granderson!*), Lion, Piston and Wing for life!

Moore Black Press Books and Authors:

jessica Care moore,
The Words Don't Fit in My Mouth

Saul Williams,
The Seventh Octave

Sharrif Simmons,
Fast Cities and Objects That Burn

jessica Care moore,
The Alphabet Verses The Ghetto

Etan Thomas,
More Than An Athlete

ras baraka,
Black Girls Learn Love Hard

asha bandele,
The Subtle Art of Breathing

Danny Simmons,
*I Dreamed My People Were Calling
But I Couldn't Find My Way Home*

*www.mooreblackpress.com
www.myspace.com/jessicacaremoore
www.myspace.com/godisnotanamerican*

192